SAMSON AGONISTES AND OTHER POEMS

William Faithorne. Portrait of John Milton at Age Sixty-Two, 1670. Graphic Arts Collection, Department of Rare Books and Special Collections, Princeton University Library. Reprinted with the permission of Princeton University Library.

SAMSON AGONISTES AND OTHER POEMS

John Milton

a *Broadview Anthology of British Literature* edition

Contributing Editor, *Samson Agonistes and Other Poems*:
Joseph Black, University of Massachusetts, Amherst

General Editors,
Broadview Anthology of British Literature:
Joseph Black, University of Massachusetts, Amherst
Leonard Conolly, Trent University
Kate Flint, University of Southern California
Isobel Grundy, University of Alberta
Don LePan, Broadview Press
Roy Liuzza, University of Tennessee
Jerome J. McGann, University of Virginia
Anne Lake Prescott, Barnard College
Barry V. Qualls, Rutgers University
Claire Waters, University of California, Davis

broadview press

Library and Archives Canada Cataloguing in Publication
Milton, John, 1608-1674
[Poems. Selections]
Samson Agonistes, and other poems / John Milton ; contributing editor, Samson Agonistes: Joseph Black, University of Massachusetts, Amherst ; general editors, Broadview Anthology of British Literature: Joseph Black, University of Massachusetts, Amherst, Leonard Conolly, Trent University, Kate Flint, University of Southern California, Isobel Grundy, University of Alberta, Don LePan, Broadview Press, Roy Liuzza, University of Tennessee, Jerome J. McGann, University of Virginia, Anne Lake Prescott, Barnard College, Barry V. Qualls, Rutgers University, Claire Waters, University of California, Davis. — A Broadview anthology of British literature edition.

In addition to Samson Agonistes, this volume includes a selection of Milton's best-known short poems, also taken from The Broadview Anthology of British Literature.
Includes bibliographical references.
ISBN 978-1-55481-209-7 (pbk.)

1. Samson (Biblical judge)—Poetry. I. Black, Joseph, 1962-, editor of compilation II. Title.

PR3552.B53 2013 821'.4 C2013-907251-9

Broadview Press is an independent, international publishing house, incorporated in 1985.

We welcome comments and suggestions regarding any aspect of our publications—please feel free to contact us at the addresses below or at broadview@broadviewpress.com.

North America	PO Box 1243, Peterborough, Ontario, Canada K9J 7H5 2215 Kenmore Ave., Buffalo, New York, USA 14207 Tel: (705) 743-8990; Fax: (705) 743-8353 email: customerservice@broadviewpress.com
UK, Europe, Central Asia, Middle East, Africa, India, and Southeast Asia	Eurospan Group, 3 Henrietta St., London WC2E 8LU, UK Tel: 44 (0) 1767 604972; Fax: 44 (0) 1767 601640 email: eurospan@turpin-distribution.com
Australia and New Zealand	NewSouth Books, c/o TL Distribution 15-23 Helles Ave., Moorebank, NSW, Australia 2170 Tel: (02) 8778 9999; Fax: (02) 8778 9944 email: orders@tldistribution.com.au

www.broadviewpress.com

Developmental Editors: Jennifer McCue and Laura Buzzard

Broadview Press acknowledges the financial support of the Government of Canada through the Canada Book Fund for our publishing activities.

This book is printed on paper containing 100% post-consumer fibre.

PRINTED IN CANADA

Contents

Introduction

John Milton

1608–1674

John Milton aspired to be a writer for the ages—and he succeeded. Almost within his lifetime, Milton was widely considered England's greatest poet and a writer whose only serious rivals were the ancient masters Homer and Virgil. His influence on subsequent English poetry is probably second only to that of Shakespeare: for centuries, major poets struggled to define themselves in relation to Milton's achievement in a literary psychodrama of admiration, emulation, exasperation, and denial. No other English writer appears to have assimilated so thoroughly all the literature, culture, and history that had come before him. Milton first mastered the European artistic tradition, and then out of it made something new, producing magnificent and innovative poems in all the major genres. In addition, had Milton not published a line of verse he would still hold a place in literary history by virtue of his prose. Even though he dismissed these books as the product of "his left hand," Milton was a significant prose writer and a formidable polemicist, in Latin as well as English, producing a wide range of works on political, social, religious, educational, and historical issues.

Of all the major writers in English, Milton was probably the most deeply engaged in the politics of his time. Milton's poetry has consequently been read in light of his active involvement in political, religious, and social revolution. But the nature of Milton's literary engagement with these issues continues to be debated: Milton, like Shakespeare, rarely if ever offers easy answers. Over the centuries, Milton has been championed as both a pillar of religious orthodoxy and as the great dissenter, a religious radical, or even heretic. He has been called a proto-feminist and the great patriarchal bogeyman, a radical political egalitarian and a man who did not believe in democracy. His is the greatest voice of "Puritanism" in English literature, but to think of him in anything like the modern sense of "puritanical" is to go immediately off-track. While a profoundly religious man, Milton by the end of his life had almost no use for institutional religion or theological tradition. While a "Puritan," he was also a spokesman for revolution, freedom of the will (which Protestant theory usually denied), and political, social, intellectual, and personal liberty. Thomas Jefferson copied out 48 excerpts from Milton's works into his commonplace book, almost all of them having to do with liberty. Milton's works have been called the culmination of Renaissance humanism and a monument to dead ideas; and they have been celebrated as ushering in the modern world in their complex treatment of human agency, human love, and human political relations.

No writer before Milton fashioned himself quite so insistently and self-consciously as an author: in text after text, Milton invites us to read connections between his life and his writing, and then challenges or complicates our ability to do so. Born the eldest son of a successful scrivener in London in 1608, Milton was surrounded by words from an early age; he began writing seriously at the age of ten. In 1618 he was admitted to Christ's College, Cambridge, where he would remain the next seven years, graduating M.A. in 1632. While Milton did very well in his studies, he also complained repeatedly about the inadequacies of the educational curriculum and requirements: he described his frustration with traditional approaches to education in his treatise *On Education* (1644). Milton entered Cambridge expecting to become a minister in the Church of England (he would later change his mind, probably in the 1630s). In his university writings, however, he talks about himself as a poet and as a scholar, but never as a prospective minister. But he did develop a reputation for erudition and literary skill: during his university years he wrote several poems he would later publish, including the companion poems "L'Allegro" and "Il Penseroso."

After he left Cambridge, Milton spent the next six years in "studious retirement," living with his parents, reading extensively, preparing himself for his vocation—and trying to discover what that vocation was.He published his first poem, an epitaph for Shakespeare included in Shakespeare's second folio (1632); he accepted commissions for two aristocratic entertainments (*Arcades* and *A Maske*, popularly known as *Comus*). He kept a close eye on the changing political and religious conditions of England over the 1630s. Finally, in 1638, he published "Lycidas," one of the most extraordinary poems in English, simultaneously a eulogy for a drowned classmate, a denunciation of current Anglican Church leadership, and a confident assertion of his own poetic vocation, all mediated through the conventions of classical pastoral elegy. Writing "Lycidas" seemed to be the trigger that propelled Milton from his retirement into an active engagement with the world. In 1638 and 1639, he traveled abroad, spending considerable time in Italy, where he was much taken with the intellectual and cultural life. Had not rumors of the impending English Civil War called him home in late 1639, Milton's travels would likely have lasted much longer.

Milton continued to train himself towards his goal of becoming a great poet in the classical tradition of Virgil, becoming familiar with Spanish, Dutch, and Hebrew as well as Latin and Greek, French and Italian, and with the leading works of history, science, and philosophy as well as of literature. But after returning to England in 1639 he devoted himself over the next twenty years very largely to the cause of political and religious change. Most of his publications during this period consist of prose polemic, including some anti-episcopal tracts in the early 1640s, several others arguing for an increased freedom to divorce, *Areopagitica* (1644), and works of political theory and argument that hold a central place among the writings of the English civil wars: *The Tenure of Kings and Magistrates* (1649), *Eikonoklastes* (1649), *Defensio pro populo Anglicano* (1651), *Defensio secunda* (1654), and *The Ready and Easy Way to Establish a Free Commonwealth* (1659). Milton's skill as a polemicist brought him to the attention of the revolutionary government, and in the 1650s he served as Secretary for Foreign Tongues in the government of Oliver Cromwell—a job that entailed writing a wide variety of official documents and letters (Latin remained the most important "foreign tongue" for international communication).

Of his prose works, the most widely read in the modern era has been *Areopagitica* (1644), Milton's extended defence of literary and intellectual freedom. The occasion for the work was the effort by Parliament to require books to be licensed prior to publication. Milton did not advocate complete freedom of the press. But his arguments for the necessity of letting readers make up their own minds, of letting arguments fight it out in the public sphere, continue to be cited in legal cases today. At the time, however, Milton was far better known, notorious even, for his books advocating a right to divorce. In June of 1642 Milton (then thirty-six) married Mary Powell, a young woman from a Royalist family. The two proved to be a less than perfect match, and she returned to her family's home in Buckinghamshire two months later. They were eventually reconciled, but many readers see a connection between their apparent difficulties and Milton's publication of *The Doctrine and Discipline of Divorce* (1642), in which he argues that the purpose of marriage is to provide companionship based on affection and like-mindedness, and that divorce should be allowed when a marriage fails to do so. The scandal Milton provoked in England with these arguments was supplanted only by the European-wide scandal he created by defending the execution of King Charles I.

While Milton might not have had time to write much poetry in the 1640s, he did publish the poetry he had written up to the outbreak of war. In 1645, a year that saw some of the bloodiest fighting of the war, Humphrey Moseley, the most prominent literary publisher of the day, produced *The Poems of Mr. John Milton, Both English and Latin*. In addition to "On the Morning of Christ's Nativity," "On Shakespeare," "L'Allegro" and "Il Penseroso," "Lycidas," and *A Maske*, the collection included twenty-two other poems in English, including ten sonnets (six of them written in Italian), and twelve Latin poems.

Milton's wife Mary died during childbirth in 1652, and one of the couple's four children died shortly thereafter. At about the same time Milton entirely lost his sight; the sonnet "When I consider how my light is spent" (often referred to as "On His Blindness") was written later that same year. His two daughters were among those who served thereafter as scribes; all of his subsequent works were dictated. In 1656 Milton married Katherine Woodcock; two years later, in 1658, she also died of complications arising from childbirth.

With the Restoration in 1660, Milton went into hiding from the authorities. Eventually he suffered a brief imprisonment, but his freedom was negotiated by friends (notable among them the poet Andrew Marvell). His existence for the final fourteen years of his life was one of relative isolation—but these were also the years of his greatest poetic achievement. Rising early each day and beginning to dictate as soon as his scribe or secretary joined him, he had begun in the late 1650s to compose *Paradise Lost*, a sweeping re-telling of the Biblical story of humanity's expulsion from Paradise; the epic was initially published in 1667 in ten books, and then reissued in a revised twelve-book edition in 1674. Since the early eighteenth century *Paradise Lost* has been almost universally accorded a central place in the English literary canon. Two other major works followed: *Paradise Regained* (1671), which presents in blank verse the story of the temptation of Jesus and of his defeat of Satan; and *Samson Agonistes* (1671), which recounts in the form of a poetic drama the story of the blind and anguished Samson, struggling to understand God's will.

In 1663 Milton married Elizabeth Minshul, who became a scribe, caregiver, and inspiration to him in the last decade of his life. Though *Paradise Lost* sold moderately well from its first publication, and though Milton came to be regarded by many as a "classic" even during his lifetime, his anti-monarchical political views precluded any official honors; when he died in 1674 he was buried not in Westminster Abbey but beside his father in Saint Giles's Church, Cripplegate.

L'Allegro[1]

Hence loathèd Melancholy
    Of Cerberus,[2] and blackest Midnight born,
In Stygian[3] cave forlorn
    'Mongst horrid shapes, and shrieks, and sights unholy,
Find out some uncouth° cell, *desolate*
    Where brooding Darkness spreads his jealous wings,
And the night-raven sings;
    There under ebon shades, and low-browed rocks,
As ragged as thy locks,
    In dark Cimmerian[4] desert ever dwell.
But come thou goddess fair and free,
In heaven yclept° Euphrosyne,[5] *named*
And by men, heart-easing Mirth,
Whom lovely Venus at a birth
With two sister Graces more
To ivy-crownèd Bacchus bore;[6]
Or whether (as some sager sing)
The frolic wind that breathes the spring,
Zephyr with Aurora[7] playing,
As he met her once a-Maying,[8]
There on beds of violets blue,
And fresh-blown roses washed in dew,
Filled her with thee a daughter fair,

---

1 *L'Allegro* Italian: The merry or happy man.

2 *Cerberus* In classical myth, the three-headed dog that guards the entrance to the underworld.

3 *Stygian* Hellishly black; from Styx, a river that in classical myth leads to the underworld.

4 *Cimmerian* Densely dark (from the Cimmerians, a people fabled in classical story to live in perpetual darkness).

5 *Euphrosyne* Classical personification of mirth and one of the three Graces.

6 *heart-easing Mirth ... Bacchus bore* Milton makes the three Graces the daughters of Venus (goddess of love) and Bacchus (god of wine); Euphrosyne's two sisters were Aglaia (Brightness) and Thalia (Bloom).

7 *Zephyr ... Aurora* Classical personifications of the west wind and of the dawn.

8 *a-Maying* Celebrating the arrival of May; May Day was celebrated with various traditional pastimes. Sterner Puritans opposed such revelry as pagan.

So buxom, blithe, and debonair.[1]
Haste thee nymph, and bring with thee
Jest and youthful Jollity,
Quips and cranks, and wanton wiles,[2]
Nods, and becks,° and wreathèd smiles, *beckonings*
Such as hang on Hebe's[3] cheek,
And love to live in dimple sleek;
Sport that wrinkled Care derides,
And Laughter holding both his sides.
Come, and trip it as ye go
On the light fantastic toe,
And in thy right hand lead with thee,
The mountain nymph, sweet Liberty;
And if I give thee honour due,
Mirth, admit me of thy crew
To live with her, and live with thee,
In unreprovèd° pleasures free; *free of blame*
To hear the lark begin his flight,
And singing startle the dull night,
From his watch-tower in the skies,
Till the dappled dawn doth rise;
Then to come in spite of sorrow,
And at my window bid good morrow,[4]
Through the sweet-briar, or the vine,
Or the twisted eglantine.
While the cock with lively din,
Scatters the rear of darkness thin,
And to the stack,° or the barn door, *haystack*
Stoutly struts his dames before,
Oft list'ning how the hounds and horn

---

1 *buxom, blithe, and debonair* These three adjectives had overlapping meanings in the period, and were often grouped with one another; *buxom* Easy-going, lively; *blithe* Merry, jolly; *debonair* Affable, kindly, gracious.

2 *Quips* Witty sayings; *cranks* Plays on words; *wanton wiles* Playful games and tricks.

3 *Hebe* Classical personification of youth.

4 *to come … bid good morrow* That is, L'Allegro comes to his window and bids the day good morrow (though some readers think it is the lark who bids good morrow to L'Allegro): the same, deliberately agentless syntax has L'Allegro "oft list'ning" and "sometime walking" in subsequent lines.

Cheerly rouse the slumb'ring morn,
From the side of some hoar° hill, *grey*
Through the high wood echoing shrill.
Sometime walking not unseen
By hedgerow elms, on hillocks green,
Right against the eastern gate,
Where the great sun begins his state,° *progress*
Robed in flames, and amber light,
The clouds in thousand liveries dight,° *clothed*
While the ploughman near at hand,
Whistles o'er the furrowed land,
And the milkmaid singeth blithe,
And the mower whets his scythe,
And every shepherd tells his tale[1]
Under the hawthorn in the dale.
Straight mine eye hath caught new pleasures
Whilst the landscape round it measures.
Russet lawns, and fallows grey,
Where the nibbling flocks do stray,
Mountains on whose barren breast
The labouring clouds do often rest:
Meadows trim with daisies pied,° *multicolored*
Shallow brooks, and rivers wide,
Towers, and battlements it sees
Bosomed high in tufted trees,
Where perhaps some beauty lies,
The cynosure[2] of neighbouring eyes.
Hard by, a cottage chimney smokes,
From betwixt two agèd oaks,
Where Corydon and Thyrsis[3] met,
Are at their savoury dinner set
Of herbs, and other country messes,° *prepared dishes*
Which the neat-handed Phyllis dresses;
And then in haste her bower she leaves,

---

1 *tells his tale* A double meaning: "tells his story" and/or "counts his flock."

2 *cynosure* Guiding star, hence center of attraction or interest.

3 *Corydon … Thyrsis* With "Phyllis" and "Thestylis" five lines below, traditional names in pastoral poetry.

With Thestylis to bind the sheaves;
Or if the earlier season lead
To the tanned° haycock in the mead, *sun-dried*
Sometimes with secure° delight *free from fear*
The upland hamlets will invite,
When the merry bells ring round,
And the jocund rebecks[1] sound
To many a youth, and many a maid,
Dancing in the chequered shade;
And young and old come forth to play
On a sunshine holiday,
Till the livelong daylight fail,
Then to the spicy nut-brown ale,
With stories told of many a feat,
How Fairy Mab[2] the junkets[3] eat,
She was pinched, and pulled she said,
And he by Friar's Lantern[4] led
Tells how the drudging Goblin[5] sweat,
To earn his cream-bowl duly set,
When in one night, ere glimpse of morn,
His shadowy flail hath threshed the corn,
That ten day-labourers could not end;
Then lies him down the lubber° fiend, *drudging*
And stretched out all the chimney's length,
Basks at the fire his hairy strength;
And crop-full[6] out of doors he flings,
Ere the first cock his matin° rings. *morning song*
Thus done the tales, to bed they creep,
By whispering winds soon lulled asleep.
Towered cities please us then,
And the busy hum of men,

---

1 *rebecks* Three-stringed fiddles.

2 *Fairy Mab* In English folklore, the Queen of the Fairies.

3 *junkets* Dishes of sweet curds and cream.

4 *Friar's Lantern* Folkloric name for the will-o'-the-wisp.

5 *Goblin* Robin Goodfellow or Hobgoblin; usually a mischievous trickster, he might help with household chores, as here, if propitiated with an offering of cream.

6 *crop-full* Filled to the brim (here, with cream).

Where throngs of knights and barons bold,
In weeds of peace[1] high triumphs hold,
With store of ladies, whose bright eyes
Rain influence, and judge the prize
Of wit, or arms, while both contend
To win her grace, whom all commend.
There let Hymen[2] oft appear
In saffron robe, with taper clear,[3]
And pomp, and feast, and revelry,
With masque, and antique pageantry,
Such sights as youthful poets dream
On summer eves by haunted stream.
Then to the well-trod stage anon,° *soon*
If Jonson's learnèd sock[4] be on,
Or sweetest Shakespeare, fancy's child,
Warble his native wood-notes wild,
And ever against eating cares,[5]
Lap me in soft Lydian airs,[6]
Married to immortal verse
Such as the meeting soul[7] may pierce
In notes, with many a winding bout° *cycle, circuit*
Of linkèd sweetness long drawn out,
With wanton heed, and giddy cunning,[8]
The melting voice through mazes running;
Untwisting all the chains that tie
The hidden soul of harmony.

---

1 *weeds of peace* Showy tournament outfits, as opposed to real, wartime armor.

2 *Hymen* Classical god of weddings.

3 *taper clear* Candle or torch; it was a good omen for the marriage if the flame burned without smoke ("clear").

4 *sock* Slipper worn by comic actors in ancient Greece (as opposed to the buskin worn by actors in tragedies): L'Allegro suggests going to the theater if one of Ben Jonson's erudite comedies is playing.

5 *eating cares* See Horace, Odes II.11.18, "Evius [Dionysus] scatters eating cares."

6 *Lydian airs* Soft, convivial songs or melodies ("Lydian" is one of the Greek musical modes).

7 *the meeting soul* I.e., the soul meeting the music.

8 *wanton heed, and giddy cunning* Two oxymorons: playful carefulness and silly, excited shrewdness.

That Orpheus self[1] may heave his head
From golden slumber on a bed
Of heaped Elysian[2] flowers, and hear
Such strains as would have won the ear
Of Pluto, to have quite set free
His half-regained Eurydice.[3]
These delights, if thou canst give,
Mirth with thee, I mean to live.

—1645 (written c. 1631–38)

Il Penseroso[4]

Hence vain deluding joys,
The brood of folly without father bred,
How little you bestead,[5]
Or fill the fixèd mind with all your toys;
Dwell in some idle brain,
And fancies fond° with gaudy shapes possess, *foolish*
As thick and numberless
As the gay motes that people the sunbeams,
Or likest hovering dreams
The fickle pensioners of Morpheus' train.[6]
But hail thou goddess, sage and holy,
Hail divinest Melancholy,

---

1 *Orpheus self* That is, Orpheus himself. For Orpheus, see note below.

2 *Elysian* From Elysian Fields or Elysium, the resting place of dead heroes in classical myth.

3 *Orpheus … Eurydice* In classical myth, Orpheus was the musician who traveled to the underworld to reclaim his wife, Eurydice, after she died. Touched by the beauty of Orpheus's playing, Pluto, god of the underworld, agreed to release her. But he made the condition that Orpheus had to leave the underworld without looking back to see if Eurydice was following; at the last minute, he looked, and lost her once again (hence she is "half-regained").

4 *Il Penseroso* Italian: The pensive or contemplative man.

5 *bestead* Help; avail; be of service.

6 *Morpheus' train* Dreams are the attendants of Morpheus, the god of sleep.

Whose saintly visage is too bright
To hit the sense of human sight;
And therefore to our weaker view,
O'erlaid with black staid Wisdom's hue.
Black, but such as in esteem, Prince
Memnon's sister[1] might beseem,
Or that starred Ethiop queen[2] that strove
To set her beauty's praise above
The sea-nymphs, and their powers offended.
Yet thou art higher far descended,
Thee bright-haired Vesta[3] long of yore,
To solitary Saturn[4] bore;
His daughter she (in Saturn's reign,
Such mixture was not held a stain°) *disgrace*
Oft in glimmering bowers, and glades
He met her, and in secret shades
Of woody Ida's[5] inmost grove,
While yet there was no fear of Jove.
Come pensive nun, devout and pure,
Sober, steadfast, and demure,
All in a robe of darkest grain,° *hue*
Flowing with majestic train,
And sable stole of cypress lawn,[6]
Over thy decent shoulders drawn.
Come, but keep thy wonted state,[7]
With even step, and musing gait,
And looks commercing° with the skies, *communicating*

---

1 *Memnon's sister* In classical myth, Memnon was an Ethiopian prince who fought on the side of the Trojans in the Trojan war; his sister was named Himera.

2 *starred Ethiop queen* Cassiopeia; in classical myth she was changed into a constellation (hence "starred") as punishment for claiming to be more beautiful than the sea nymphs.

3 *Vesta* Classical goddess of hearth and home.

4 *Saturn* In classical myth, father of Jove (mentioned below); traditionally "solitary," he was associated with melancholics (hence the adjective "saturnine") even though his was the Golden Age.

5 *Ida* Mount Ida, in Crete, the traditional site from which Saturn ruled, before his son Jove overthrew him.

6 *cypress lawn* Lawn is a fine linen, usually white, but "cypress lawn" is black.

7 *wonted state* Usual dignity.

Thy rapt soul sitting in thine eyes:
There held in holy passion still,
Forget thyself to marble, till
With a sad leaden downward cast,
Thou fix them on the earth as fast.
And join with thee calm Peace, and Quiet,
Spare Fast, that oft with gods doth diet,
And hears the Muses in a ring,
Ay round about Jove's altar sing.
And add to these retired Leisure,
That in trim gardens takes his pleasure;
But first, and chiefest, with thee bring,
Him that yon soars on golden wing,
Guiding the fiery-wheelèd throne,[1]
The cherub Contemplation,[2]
And the mute Silence hist° along, *summon*
'Less Philomel[3] will deign a song,
In her sweetest, saddest plight,
Smoothing the rugged brow of night,
While Cynthia[4] checks her dragon yoke,
Gently o'er th' accustomed° oak; *usual*
Sweet bird that shunn'st the noise of folly,
Most musical, most melancholy!
Thee chauntress° oft the woods among, *female singer*
I woo to hear thy even-song;
And missing thee, I walk unseen
On the dry smooth-shaven green,
To behold the wandering moon,
Riding near her highest noon,[5]

---

1 *fiery-wheelèd throne* Apparently referring to the Biblical vision of Ezekiel (Ezekiel 10) of a chariot guided by cherubim (angels).

2 *The cherub Contemplation* The cherubim are angels, second in the nine ranks of celestial hierarchy; their special faculty is contemplation of God.

3 *Philomel* The nightingale, from a classical story in which a young woman, Philomela, is transformed into the sweet-singing bird after being raped and silenced by having her tongue cut out (hence "saddest plight").

4 *Cynthia* Classical goddess of the moon, here imagined as driving across the night sky in a chariot drawn by a dragon.

5 *highest noon* Highest point, apogee.

Like one that had been led astray
Through the heaven's wide pathless way;
And oft, as if her head she bowed,
Stooping through a fleecy cloud.
Oft on a plat° of rising ground, *patch*
I hear the far-off curfew sound,[1]
Over some wide-watered shore,
Swinging slow with sullen roar;
Or if the air will not permit,
Some still removèd place will fit,
Where glowing embers through the room
Teach light to counterfeit a gloom,
Far from all resort of mirth,
Save the cricket on the hearth,
Or the bellman's° drowsy charm, *night watchman*
To bless the doors from nightly harm:
Or let my lamp at midnight hour,
Be seen in some high lonely tower,
Where I may oft outwatch the Bear,[2]
With thrice great Hermes,[3] or unsphere
The spirit of Plato[4] to unfold
What worlds, or what vast regions hold
The immortal mind that hath forsook
Her mansion in this fleshly nook:
And of those daemons[5] that are found
In fire, air, flood, or underground,
Whose power hath a true consent
With planet, or with element.
Sometime let gorgeous Tragedy

---

1 *curfew sound* Bells rung to signal the beginning of restrictions on nighttime activity.

2 *the Bear* The constellation Ursa Major.

3 *thrice great Hermes* Hermes Trismegistus, the reputed author of the classical *Corpus Hermeticum*, a collection of mystical ("Hermetic") writings that Il Penseroso stays up all night to read.

4 *unsphere ... Plato* Il Penseroso contemplates reading the works of Plato, whose spirit is imagined as inhabiting a heavenly sphere or star.

5 *daemons* From neo-Platonic or Hermetic philosophy, spirits that inhabit the four "elements" of fire, air, water, and earth.

In sceptred pall[1] come sweeping by,
Presenting Thebes, or Pelops' line,[2]
Or the tale of Troy divine.
Or what (though rare) of later age,
Ennobled hath the buskined stage.[3]
But, O sad virgin, that thy power
Might raise Musaeus[4] from his bower,
Or bid the soul of Orpheus sing
Such notes as warbled to the string,
Drew iron tears down Pluto's cheek,
And made hell grant what love did seek.[5]
Or call up him[6] that left half-told
The story of Cambuscan bold,
Of Camball, and of Algarsife,
And who had Canace to wife,
That owned the virtuous ring and glass,
And of the wondrous horse of brass,
On which the Tartar king did ride;[7]
And if aught else, great bards beside,
In sage and solemn tunes have sung,
Of tourneys and of trophies hung;
Of forest, and enchantments drear,

---

1 *sceptred pall* Cloak and trappings of royalty.

2 *Thebes, or Pelops' line* Two royal families whose stories provided subject matter for classical tragedies: the house of Thebes was that of Oedipus and his family; the house of Pelops was the family of Atreus, Agamemnon, Orestes, Electra, and Iphigenia.

3 *buskined stage* Tragedies, from the footwear worn by Greek tragic actors; Milton implies that good tragedies were rare in his (as opposed to the classical) period.

4 *Musaeus* In classical myth, a great singer, sometimes called the son of Orpheus.

5 *Orpheus … seek* In classical myth, Orpheus was the master musician who traveled to the underworld to reclaim his wife, Eurydice, after she died. Touched by the beauty of Orpheus's playing, Pluto, god of the underworld, agreed to release her. But he made the condition that Orpheus had to leave the underworld without looking back to see if Eurydice was following; at the last minute, he looked, and lost her once again.

6 *him* I.e., Geoffrey Chaucer.

7 *story of … ride* The romance of Cambuscan, his children Camball, Algarsife, and Canace, and the gifts of a brass horse and a magic ring, is told in Chaucer's unfinished "Squire's Tale" in the *Canterbury Tales*, and continued by Spenser in Book 4 of *The Faerie Queene*.

Where more is meant than meets the ear.[1]
Thus Night oft see me in thy pale career,
Till civil-suited Morn appear,
Not tricked and frounced[2] as she was wont,
With the Attic boy[3] to hunt,
But kerchiefed in a comely° cloud, *attractive*
While rocking winds are piping loud,
Or ushered with a shower still,
When the gust hath blown his fill,
Ending on the rustling leaves,
With minute drops from off the eaves.
And when the sun begins to fling
His flaring beams, me goddess bring
To archèd walks of twilight groves,
And shadows brown that Sylvan[4] loves
Of pine, or monumental oak,
Where the rude axe with heavèd stroke,
Was never heard the nymphs to daunt,
Or fright them from their hallowed haunt.
There in close covert° by some brook, *hidden shelter*
Where no profaner eye may look,
Hide me from day's garish eye,
While the bee with honied thigh,
That at her flowery work doth sing,
And the waters murmuring
With such consort° as they keep, *agreement, harmony*
Entice the dewy-feathered Sleep;
And let some strange mysterious dream,
Wave at his wings in airy stream,
Of lively portraiture displayed,
Softly on my eyelids laid.
And as I wake, sweet music breathe

---

1 *more is meant than meets the ear* Reference to *The Faerie Queene* and Spenser's allegorical method.

2 *civil-suited Morn … and frounced* Soberly dressed, without showy clothes or hairstyle.

3 *Attic boy* In classical myth, Aurora (Dawn) loved Cephalus, an Athenian (Attic) youth.

4 *Sylvan* Sylvanus, Roman god of forests.

Above, about, or underneath,
Sent by some spirit to mortals good,
Or th' unseen genius° of the wood. *guardian spirit*
But let my due° feet never fail, *dutiful*
To walk the studious cloister's[1] pale,° *enclosure*
And love the high embowèd° roof, *arched*
With antique pillars' massy proof,° *solidity*
And storied windows[2] richly dight,° *decorated*
Casting a dim religious light.
There let the pealing organ blow,
To the full-voiced choir below,
In service high, and anthems clear,
As may with sweetness, through mine ear,
Dissolve me into ecstasies,
And bring all heaven before mine eyes.
And may at last my weary age
Find out the peaceful hermitage,
The hairy gown and mossy cell,
Where I may sit and rightly spell,[3]
Of every star that heaven doth shew,
And every herb that sips the dew;
Till old experience do attain
To something like prophetic strain.
These pleasures Melancholy give,
And I with thee will choose to live.

—1645 (written c.1631–38)

---

1 *cloister* Covered walk; here, probably a university, not a monastic, cloister.
2 *storied windows* Pictorial stained glass windows.
3 *spell* Study, decipher.

Lycidas

In this monody[1] the author bewails a learned friend,[2] unfortunately drowned in his passage from Chester on the Irish Seas, 1637. And by occasion foretells the ruin of our corrupted clergy then in their height.[3]

Yet once more, O ye laurels, and once more
Ye myrtles brown, with ivy never sere,° *withered*
I come to pluck your berries harsh and crude,° *unripe*
And with forced fingers rude,
Shatter your leaves before the mellowing year.[4]
Bitter constraint, and sad occasion dear,
Compels me to disturb your season due:
For Lycidas[5] is dead, dead ere his prime,
Young Lycidas, and hath not left his peer:
Who would not sing for Lycidas? he knew
Himself to sing, and build the lofty rhyme.
He must not float upon his watery bier[6]
Unwept, and welter[7] to the parching wind,
Without the meed° of some melodious tear. *honor*

---

1 *monody* Lament sung by one voice.

2 *friend* Edward King (1612–37), a fellow student of Milton's at Cambridge.

3 *In this ... height* Milton added this headnote to the version in his *Poems* (1645), published when the success of Parliament in the Civil Wars made it possible to publish a comment about the "corrupted clergy." When the poem was first published, in a 1638 collection of poems dedicated to the memory of Edward King, English bishops under the leadership of Archbishop William Laud were indeed at the "height" of their power.

4 *laurels ... mellowing year* The three evergreens mentioned here were emblems of poetic achievement: laurel was sacred to Apollo, so a laurel wreath was the traditional crown of poets; myrtle was sacred to Venus, and so was an emblem of love poetry; ivy was linked with Bacchus, god of wine, and so was associated with poetic ecstasy or inspiration. By saying that he needs to pluck these berries before they are ripe, the speaker implies that he thinks himself unready to write the poetry these plants honored.

5 *Lycidas* Traditional name in classical and Renaissance pastoral literature.

6 *bier* Framework or stand on which a corpse or coffin is placed.

7 *welter* Roll or tumble about.

Begin then, sisters of the sacred well,[1]
That from beneath the seat of Jove[2] doth spring,
Begin, and somewhat loudly sweep the string.
Hence with denial vain, and coy excuse,
So may some gentle muse
With lucky words favour my destined urn,
And as he passes turn,
And bid fair peace be to my sable° shroud. *black*
For we were nursed upon the self-same hill,[3]
Fed the same flock; by fountain, shade, and rill.° *brook*
Together both, ere the high lawns[4] appeared
Under the opening eyelids of the morn,
We drove afield, and both together heard
What time the grey-fly winds[5] her sultry horn,
Battening° our flocks with the fresh dews[6] of night, *feeding*
Oft till the star that rose, at evening, bright
Toward heaven's descent had sloped his westering wheel.
Meanwhile the rural ditties were not mute,
Tempered° to the oaten flute, *attuned*
Rough satyrs[7] danced, and fauns with cloven heel,
From the glad sound would not be absent long,
And old Damoetas[8] loved to hear our song.
But O the heavy change, now thou art gone,
Now thou art gone, and never must return!
Thee shepherd, thee the woods, and desert caves,
With wild thyme and the gadding° vine o'ergrown, *rambling*

---

1 *sisters of the sacred well* The nine Muses; their well is the emblematic source of artistic inspiration.

2 *seat of Jove* Probably Mt. Olympus, from beneath which one of the muses' sacred springs flowed; possibly Mt. Helicon, the site of another sacred spring.

3 *nursed upon the self-same hill* Milton uses pastoral conventions to indicate that he and "Lycidas" went to the same school.

4 *lawns* Open spaces between woods, glades.

5 *winds* Blows its horn (that is, buzzes).

6 *dews* Grasses still covered in dew.

7 *satyrs* Part human, part animal creatures associated with lechery and wildness; when translated from the pastoral fiction, these are Milton's fellow undergraduates at Cambridge.

8 *Damoetas* Conventional pastoral name, and here a teacher or mentor figure, possibly alluding to a real tutor at Cambridge.

And all their echoes mourn.
The willows, and the hazel copses green,
Shall now no more be seen,
Fanning their joyous leaves to thy soft lays.° *songs*
As killing as the canker[1] to the rose,
Or taint-worm to the weanling herds[2] that graze,
Or frost to flowers, that their gay wardrobe wear,
When first the whitethorn blows;° *blooms*
Such, Lycidas, thy loss to shepherd's ear.
 Where were ye nymphs when the remorseless deep
Closed o'er the head of your loved Lycidas?
For neither were ye playing on the steep,° *mountain*
Where your old bards, the famous Druids[3] lie,
Nor on the shaggy top of Mona high,
Nor yet where Deva spreads her wizard stream:
Ay me, I fondly° dream! *foolishly*
Had ye been there—for what could that have done?
What could the Muse herself that Orpheus bore,
The Muse herself, for her enchanting son
Whom universal nature did lament,
When by the rout that made the hideous roar,
His gory visage down the stream was sent,
Down the swift Hebrus to the Lesbian shore.[4]
 Alas! What boots° it with uncessant care *profits*
To tend the homely° slighted[5] shepherd's trade, *humble*
And strictly meditate the thankless Muse,
Were it not better done as others use,

---

1 *canker* Fungal disease of plants.

2 *taint-worm to the weanling herds* Intestinal parasite afflicting lambs or calves (weanlings).

3 *Druids* The speaker asks if the sea nymphs failed to save King because they were playing in places associated with the Druids, ancient Celtic minstrel-poets or, here, "bards": Bardsey (the "steep" island where they "lie" buried), the island of Mona (Anglesey), and the river Dee (here, Latinized as "Deva") in Chester.

4 *What could the Muse … shore* Orpheus was the greatest musician/poet in the classical tradition; his mother was the Muse Calliope. He met his death at the hands of Maenads, a group of women in an ecstatic frenzy. Orpheus's severed bleeding head ("gory visage") floated down the Hebrus river across the sea and to the island of Lesbos, where the Muses buried it.

5 *slighted* Treated with disrespect.

To sport with Amaryllis in the shade,
Or with the tangles of Neaera's[1] hair?
Fame is the spur that the clear spirit doth raise
(That last infirmity of noble mind)
To scorn delights, and live laborious days;
But the fair guerdon° when we hope to find, *reward*
And think to burst out into sudden blaze,
Comes the blind Fury[2] with th' abhorrèd shears,
And slits the thin-spun life. But not the praise,
Phoebus[3] replied, and touched my trembling ears;
Fame is no plant that grows on mortal soil,
Nor in the glistering foil[4]
Set off to the world, nor in broad rumour lies,
But lives and spreads aloft by those pure eyes,
And perfect witness of all-judging Jove;
As he pronounces lastly on each deed,
Of so much fame in heaven expect thy meed.° *reward*
    O fountain Arethuse,[5] and thou honoured flood,
Smooth-sliding Mincius[6] crowned with vocal reeds,
That strain° I heard was of a higher mood: *melody*
But now my oat[7] proceeds,
And listens to the herald of the sea° *Triton*
That came in Neptune's plea,
He asked the waves, and asked the felon winds,
What hard mishap hath doomed this gentle swain?
And questioned every gust of rugged wings[8]

---

1 *Amaryllis ... Neaera* Conventional names in pastoral poetry for young women.

2 *Fury* In classical myth, the three Fates respectively spun the thread of life, measured it, and then cut it; the Fate with the cutting shears was named Atropos, or Destiny. The speaker compares her to one of the Furies, another group of mythological sisters, who were snaky-haired agents of vengeance.

3 *Phoebus* Apollo, god of poetry.

4 *glistering foil* Glittering layer of polished metal placed under a gem to lend it brilliance or under a glass mirror to aid reflectivity.

5 *Arethuse* Fountain on an island near Sicily, associated with pastoral poetry; named for the nymph Arethusa, who was transformed into the fountain while being chased by the river god Alpheus (see below, line 132).

6 *Mincius* River in Mantua, where the Roman poet Virgil was born.

7 *oat* Oaten flute (of l. 33); metaphorically, the speaker's song (poem).

8 *wings* Winds, imagined as birdlike.

That blows from off each beakèd° promontory; *pointed*
They knew not of his story,
And sage Hippotades[1] their answer brings,
That not a blast was from his dungeon strayed,
The air was calm, and on the level brine,
Sleek Panope[2] with all her sisters played.
It was that fatal and perfidious bark° *ship*
Built in th' eclipse, and rigged with curses dark,
That sunk so low that sacred head of thine.
    Next Camus,[3] reverend sire, went footing slow,
His mantle hairy, and his bonnet sedge,[4]
Inwrought with figures dim, and on the edge
Like to that sanguine flower inscribed with woe.[5]
Ah! who hath reft (quoth he) my dearest pledge?[6]
Last came, and last did go,
The pilot of the Galilean lake,[7]
Two massy keys he bore of metals twain
(The golden opes, the iron shuts amain°), *forcefully*
He shook his mitred locks,[8] and stern bespake,
How well could I have spared for thee, young swain,
Enow° of such as for their bellies' sake, *enough*
Creep and intrude, and climb into the fold?° *sheepfold*
Of other care they little reckoning make,
Than how to scramble at the shearers' feast,

---

1 *Hippotades* Aeolus, the classical keeper of winds.

2 *Panope* The chief nymph of fifty sea-nymph sisters, the Nereids.

3 *Camus* Personification of the River Cam, in Cambridge.

4 *His mantle hairy, and his bonnet sedge* His cloak was coarsely woven, and his hat was woven of reeds.

5 *sanguine flower ... woe* The hyacinth. In classical myth, it sprang from the blood of Hyacinthus, a youth beloved of Apollo; the god recorded his grief by marking the flower with the letters AI AI ("alas").

6 *who hath reft ... dearest pledge?* Who has stolen Camus's dearest initiate?

7 *pilot of the Galilean lake* Usually identified as St. Peter, speaking as the founder of the Christian Church; he mourns the loss of a young man who had intended to enter the ministry. He holds the keys of the kingdom of Heaven (from Matthew 16.19). The pilot is sometimes identified as Christ. But as a (ship) pilot on Galilee, Peter would here appear to be paired with Christ, mentioned in line 173 below as "Him that walked the waves."

8 *mitred locks* Peter, the first bishop, wears the bishop's miter (a tall, cleft headdress), and shakes his head.

And shove away the worthy bidden guest.
Blind mouths! that scarce themselves know how to hold
A sheep-hook, or have learned aught else the least
That to the faithful herdman's art belongs!
What recks it them?[1] What need they? They are sped;[2]
And when they list,[3] their lean and flashy songs
Grate on their scrannel[4] pipes of wretched straw,
The hungry sheep look up, and are not fed,
But swoll'n with wind, and the rank mist they draw,° *breathe*
Rot inwardly, and foul contagion spread:
Besides what the grim wolf[5] with privy paw[6]
Daily devours apace, and nothing said,[7]
But that two-handed engine[8] at the door,
Stands ready to smite once, and smite no more.
Return Alpheus,[9] the dread voice is past,
That shrunk thy streams; return Sicilian Muse,[10]
And call the vales, and bid them hither cast
Their bells, and flowrets of a thousand hues.
Ye valleys low where the mild whispers use,° *frequent*

---

1 *What recks it them* What do they care?

2 *They are sped* They have done well.

3 *when they list* When they choose, or please.

4 *scrannel* Shriveled, thin; an unusual word, probably provincial dialect, apparently chosen for its appropriately ugly sound.

5 *wolf* Usually identified as an allusion to the threat posed by Catholicism.

6 *with privy paw* With secret or hidden steps; possibly also an allusion to the Privy Council, and implying that the government under Charles I was helping the Church push a Catholic agenda.

7 *nothing said* In the manuscript version of this poem, Milton originally wrote "nothing" but then crossed it out and wrote "little"; "nothing" appears in the 1645 edition.

8 *two-handed engine* The specific reference here continues to be debated. Probably, in one respect, a sword: in *Paradise Lost*, the Archangel Michael wields a "huge two-handed" sword (6.251), which likely refers to the two-edged swords mentioned in Revelation 1.16 and Psalm 149.6. But as an emblem for divine agency or judgment, the "sword of God" can also be interpreted as manifesting itself in many different objects, institutions, or ideas (such as the two keys of line 110 above).

9 *Alpheus* River in Greece, and the god of the river (see l. 85 above). The speaker invites the return of sources that inspire the pastoral mode.

10 *Sicilian Muse* Probably Arethusa (see l. 85 above). Sicily was associated with the pastoral mode: the poet Theocritus (fl. 280 BCE), the creator of pastoral poetry, was Sicilian.

Of shades and wanton winds, and gushing brooks,
On whose fresh lap the swart star[1] sparely looks,
Throw hither all your quaint enamelled eyes,
That on the green turf suck the honied showers,
And purple all the ground with vernal° flowers. *spring*
Bring the rathe° primrose that forsaken dies, *early blooming*
The tufted crow-toe, and pale jessamine,
The white pink, and the pansy freaked° with jet, *streaked*
The glowing violet,
The musk-rose, and the well-attired woodbine,
With cowslips wan that hang the pensive head,
And every flower that sad embroidery wears:
Bid amaranthus all his beauty shed,
And daffodillies fill their cups with tears,
To strew the laureate[2] hearse where Lycid lies.
For so to interpose a little ease,
Let our frail thoughts dally with false surmise
(Ay me!) Whilst thee the shores, and sounding seas
Wash far away, where'er thy bones are hurled,
Whether beyond the stormy Hebrides
Where thou perhaps under the whelming tide
Visit'st the bottom of the monstrous world;
Or whether thou to our moist vows denied,
Sleep'st by the fable of Bellerus[3] old,
Where the great vision of the guarded mount[4]
Looks toward Namancos and Bayona's hold;° *fortress*
Look homeward angel now, and melt with ruth.° *pity*
And, O ye dolphins, waft the hapless youth.
    Weep no more, woeful shepherds weep no more,
For Lycidas your sorrow is not dead,
Sunk though he be beneath the watery floor,

---

1 *swart star* Sirius, the Dog Star, associated with the hottest weeks of the year and called "swart" because the hot weather of summer darkens the complexion.

2 *laureate* Decorated with laurel (see line 1).

3 *Bellerus* Milton apparently invents the name from Bellarium, the Latin name for Land's End in Cornwall, the south-west tip of England.

4 *guarded mount* St. Michael's Mount in Cornwall, from which the Archangel was traditionally said to guard England; here, Michael looks out toward two places in Spain, but is asked to look "homeward" in pity for Lycidas.

So sinks the day-star° in the ocean bed, *the sun*
And yet anon° repairs his drooping head, *soon*
And tricks his beams, and with new spangled ore,[1]
Flames in the forehead of the morning sky:
So Lycidas sunk low, but mounted high,
Through the dear might of him[2] that walked the waves,
Where other groves, and other streams along,
With nectar pure his oozy locks he laves,° *washes*
And hears the unexpressive° nuptial song, *inexpressible*
In the blest kingdoms meek° of joy and love. *gentle*
There entertain him all the saints above,
In solemn troops, and sweet societies
That sing, and singing in their glory move,
And wipe the tears for ever from his eyes.
Now Lycidas the shepherds weep no more;
Henceforth thou art the genius° of the shore, *guardian spirit*
In thy large recompense, and shalt be good
To all that wander in that perilous flood.
    Thus sang the uncouth° swain to th' oaks and rills, *unknown*
While the still morn went out with sandals grey,
He touched the tender stops of various quills,° *reeds (flutes)*
With eager thought warbling his Doric[3] lay:
And now the sun had stretched out all the hills,
And now was dropped into the western bay;
At last he rose, and twitched° his mantle blue:[4] *tossed on*
Tomorrow to fresh woods, and pastures new.[5]

—1638, 1645

---

1 *tricks his beams ... ore* The sun adorns its beams with fresh gold.

2 *him* Christ (Matthew 14.25-31).

3 *Doric* Musical mode.

4 *blue* Color traditionally associated with hope.

5 *Thus sang ... new* The final eight lines, rhyming ABABABCC, reflect the form of an *ottava rima* stanza, one pattern associated with epic narrative poetry.

Sonnets

7

How soon hath Time the subtle thief of youth,
Stol'n on his wing my three and twenti'th year!
My hasting days fly on with full career,
But my late spring no bud or blossom shew'th.° *shows*
Perhaps my semblance might deceive the truth,
That I to manhood am arriv'd so near,
And inward ripeness doth much less appear,
That some more timely-happy spirits endu'th.° *endows*
Yet be it less or more, or soon or slow,
It shall be still° in strictest measure ev'n, *always*
To that same lot, however mean, or high,
Toward which Time leads me, and the will of Heav'n;
All is, if I have grace to use it so,
As ever in my great task-master's eye.

—1645 (written either 1631 or 1632)

16[1]

To the Lord General Cromwell[2]

Cromwell, our chief of men, who through a cloud
Not of war only, but detractions rude,
Guided by faith and matchless fortitude,
To peace and truth thy glorious way hast ploughed,
And on the neck of crowned Fortune proud
Hast reared God's trophies, and his work pursued,

1 *16* Not published in Milton's lifetime. It is numbered sonnet 16 in Milton's manuscript version, though some modern editions give the number 16 to "When I consider how my light is spent" (Sonnet 19 here). The manuscript dates the poem May 1652, and has a scratched-out subtitle: "On the proposals of certain ministers at the Committee for Propagation of the Gospel."

2 *To the Lord General Cromwell* Oliver Cromwell (1599–1658), at the time Commander-in-Chief of the Parliamentary Army, and subsequently Lord Protector.

While Darwen stream[1] with blood of Scots
imbrued,° *permeated*
And Dunbar field[2] resounds thy praises loud,
And Worcester's[3] laureate wreath; yet much remains
To conquer still: peace hath her victories
No less renown'd than war. New foes arise
Threat'ning to bind our souls with secular chains:[4]
Help us to save free conscience from the paw
Of hireling[5] wolves whose Gospel is their maw.

—1694 (written 1652)

18[6]

On the Late Massacre in Piedmont[7]

Avenge O Lord thy slaughtered saints,[8] whose bones
Lie scattered on the Alpine mountains cold,
Even them who kept thy truth so pure of old
When all our fathers worshipped stocks and stones,
Forget not: in thy book record their groans
Who were thy sheep and in their ancient fold

---

1 *Darwen stream* The river near Preston, where Cromwell defeated a Scottish army in August 1648.

2 *Dunbar field* Where Cromwell routed the Scottish army in September 1650.

3 *Worcester* Where Cromwell in 1651 defeated the Royalist Army of Charles II, who was crowned in Scotland when in exile after the death of his father.

4 *To conquer … secular chains* Referring to the proposals mentioned in the poem's manuscript subtitle (see note above) that sought to reinstall a state-controlled church.

5 *hireling* Milton disapproved of compulsory tithes, believing that congregations should be able to hire ministers of their own choosing: to him, ministers in a state church are hired state employees.

6 *18* Some modern editions number this sonnet 15, the number assigned it in the 1673 edition of Milton's *Poems.*

7 *Massacre in Piedmont* In April 1655, a Catholic army under the command of the Duke of Savoy began a persecution of the Vaudois or Waldensians, a Protestant sect that lived in the mountainous Piedmont region of Italy, near the Swiss border. The Waldensians had broken away from the Catholic Church in the twelfth century. But seventeenth-century Protestants thought they represented a much older tradition, and regarded them as having retained the beliefs of the primitive Church.

8 *saints* The term "saint" can refer not only to a martyr or one who has been canonized, but also to any believer in Christ. See, e.g., 1 Corinthians 1.2, 2 Corinthians 1.1, and Romans 1.7.

Slain by the bloody Piedmontese that rolled
Mother with infant down the rocks. Their moans
The vales redoubled to the hills, and they
To Heaven. Their martyred blood and ashes sow
O'er all the Italian fields where still doth sway
The triple tyrant:[1] that from these may grow
A hundredfold, who having learnt thy way
Early may fly the Babylonian[2] woe.

—1673 (written 1655)

19[3]

When I consider how my light is spent,
Ere half my days,[4] in this dark world and wide,
And that one talent[5] which is death to hide,
Lodged with me useless, though my soul more bent
To serve therewith my maker, and present
My true account, lest he returning chide,
Doth God exact day-labour, light denied,
I fondly° ask; but patience to prevent *foolishly*
That murmur, soon replies, God doth not need
Either man's work or his own gifts, who best
Bear his mild yoke, they serve him best; his state
Is kingly. Thousands[6] at his bidding speed
And post° o'er land and ocean without rest: *ride*
They also serve who only stand and wait.

—1673 (probably written 1652)

---

1 *triple tyrant* The pope, from the three-crowned papal miter or headdress.

2 *Babylonian* Protestants of Milton's time often used Babylon as a metaphor for the excesses of the papal court.

3 *19* Numbered sonnet 16 in some modern editions. The title "On his blindness" was added in the eighteenth century, and appears in some modern editions.

4 *half my days* The source of much debate on the date of this poem: Milton was born in December 1608, and it is not clear by what standard he judges the normal length of a life. He was totally blind by early 1652.

5 *talent* Alluding to the parable of the talents in Matthew 25.14-30.

6 *Thousands* I.e., thousands of angels.

23[1]

Methought I saw my late espoused saint[2]
Brought to me, like Alcestis,[3] from the grave,
Whom Jove's great son to her glad husband gave,
Rescued from death by force, though pale and faint.
Mine, as whom washed from spot of child-bed taint
Purification in the old Law[4] did save,
And such as yet once more I trust to have
Full sight of her in Heaven without restraint,
Came vested all in white, pure as her mind;
Her face was veiled,[5] yet to my fancied sight
Love, sweetness, goodness in her person shined
So clear as in no face with more delight.
But O as to embrace me she inclined,
I waked, she fled, and day brought back my night.

—1673 (date of composition unknown)

---

1 *23* Numbered sonnet 19 in some modern editions.

2 *late espoused saint* Milton's first wife, Mary Powell, died in May 1652, shortly after giving birth to their daughter Deborah. His second wife, Katherine Woodcock, died in February 1658, several months after giving birth to their daughter Katherine. Most scholars believe that the poem refers to Katherine, though arguments have been made for Mary as its subject.

3 *Alcestis* In classical myth, Alcestis sacrificed her life to save her husband, Admetus; Hercules, the son of Jove, repays Admetus's hospitality to him by forcing Death (in a wrestling match) to return her alive. The story is told in the play *Alcestis* by Euripedes.

4 *Purification in the old Law* Referring to the rites of purification after childbirth detailed in Leviticus 12 (the old Law of the Old Testament, as opposed to the new Law of the New Testament).

5 *veiled* Like Alcestis, when she returned; but also from the reader.

Samson Agonistes

The biblical story of Samson seems an almost inevitable subject for Milton to address after the Restoration of 1660, when England abandoned its experiment in republicanism and welcomed back both the monarchy and the state church. Samson's initial situation in the poem echoes repeatedly with Milton's likely sense of his own situation: blind and no longer in a position of power; ruled by an enemy with an entertainment-loving aristocracy, politically powerful clergy, and emptily ceremonial religion; disappointed in his countrymen because they preferred "bondage with ease" over "strenuous liberty" (line 271); and questioning his apparent failure to fulfill his divinely appointed role of national liberator. *Samson Agonistes* (1671) addresses matters that Milton had explored throughout *Paradise Lost* (1667) and other works, questions that pressed insistently on the imagination of all who were unhappy with the changes wrought by the Restoration. How do we respond to the experience of defeat, and to fears of having been abandoned by the divine? How do we know when our actions accord with divine will, or when they are fueled instead by our fallen desires and weaknesses? At what point do accommodation and compromise with an enemy become a failure of will? What constitutes true heroism? To what extent is violence justified in the cause of freedom?

Samson Agonistes was first published in a volume with *Paradise Regained* in 1671, four years after the first edition of *Paradise Lost.* While there was some speculation decades ago that *Samson Agonistes* was written before *Paradise Lost*, the consensus now overwhelmingly favors a date of composition in the later 1660s, after Milton had completed both *Paradise Lost* and *Paradise Regained.* Scholars note that *Samson Agonistes* appears to contain several topical allusions to post-Restoration events, and that the poem engages throughout with the language of Restoration debates on political and religious accommodation. Furthermore, its daringly experimental prosody suggests that Milton wrote the poem late in his career. In *Samson Agonistes*, Milton abandons the regularly maintained blank verse of *Paradise Lost* and *Paradise Regained* and employs varying line lengths, mixes blank verse with lyric rhyme, and takes such liberties with scansion that the poem often has the feel of modern "free verse." To most scholars, the poetry of *Samson Agonistes* seems the culminating literary expression of a poet who had already demonstrated his mastery of traditional forms and felt free to abandon convention to create the poetic effects he desired. Finally, for many readers as well as scholars, the resonant last line of *Samson Agonistes*—"And calm of mind all passion spent"—offers a cathartic conclusion to a literary career devoted to passionate engagement with the most fundamental aspects of the human condition.

As Milton notes in his preface, *Samson Agonistes* is a "dramatic poem": while it takes the form of drama, specifically of ancient Greek tragedy, and has been performed successfully in staged readings, it was never intended for the stage. The poem opens with Samson already blinded and enslaved, bemoaning his condition, questioning the events that had reduced him to such a pitiful state. He reminds us that he had once been a great warrior, consecrated to God from birth and divinely appointed to deliver Israel from its bondage under the Philistines. But he had betrayed the secret of his unconquerable strength to his Philistine wife Dalila, and she in turn had betrayed him to the Philistines once she had rendered him temporarily powerless by cutting his hair. A series of discussions then ensues between Samson and various visitors: a Chorus of fellow tribesmen, his wife Dalila, his father Manoa, the Philistine giant Harapha, and a Public Officer. The poem ends when Samson is commanded to entertain his captors by performing feats of strength at a religious festival; he concludes his performance by pulling down the building's pillars, killing himself along with the Philistine social, political, military, and religious elite. As in Greek tragedy, the concluding violence takes place offstage and is reported by a messenger.

Milton freely expands on the biblical account, adding and omitting details, telling the story in his own way for his own purposes. But what these purposes might be is a question that has generated considerable debate. To many modern readers, the biblical Samson can seem more a thuggish trickster figure from folklore than a proper national hero. A long tradition of Christian commentary, however, has interpreted Samson as a prefiguration of Christ, a "type" of the self-sacrificing and regenerate savior. Is that how Milton presents him? While some scholars argue that *Samson Agonistes* offers an unambiguous drama of spiritual regeneration, others argue instead that Milton's Samson is a failed Old Testament hero whose actions contrast with the true heroism of Jesus in *Paradise Regained*, the poem with which *Samson Agonistes* was originally published. One difficulty of *Samson Agonistes* is that Milton's choice of the dramatic form deprives readers of the helpfully omniscient narrative voices of *Paradise Lost* or the Bible. Did God really give "to the man despotic power / Over his female in due awe" (lines 1054–55), as the Chorus claims, or is it more the case, as Dalila notes, that "In argument with men a woman ever / Goes by the worse, whatever be her cause" (lines 903–04)? Each claim is self-evidently true to its speaker, but the poem requires readers to judge between them. When Samson feels "Some rousing motions" within himself (line 1382) as he heads toward suicidal slaughter, are readers confident that his actions are prompted by God? The biblical account makes divine approval explicit; in Milton's presentation, Samson's sudden and unexplained shift in strategy may invite questions. Similarly, when the Messenger describes Samson as inclining his head "as one who prayed" (line 1637), is Samson praying, or simply inclining his head *like* somebody who prays? If Samson's violence is divinely justified, why does Milton take such care to make the slaughter more socially selective than it was in the biblical account? Is the poem ultimately a call to revolution, a vindication of revolution, or a repudiation of revolution?

The heated struggles of scholars with this poem and with one another fittingly reflect the poem's central subject: Samson's struggle to understand himself. "Agonistes" is the Greek word for an athlete competing in the Olympic games, and Milton's appropriation of the word for use in a biblical context adds the resonance of Christian spiritual struggle as well as the physical agonies of Christ. In addition, "agon" was the term used in ancient Greek drama for a verbal contest between two characters. In each "agon" or dialogic encounter with a figure from his life, Samson also struggles with some element within himself: the voice of tribal wisdom in the Chorus, the fame-loving sensualist in Dalila, the strong man who delights in violence in Harapha, the compromiser in his father Manoa. Because the dramatic form gives each visitor his or her say without explicit narratorial framing, the reader consequently spends the poem in Samson's position. We too are blind, reliant on the Chorus to introduce us to each visitor; we listen to and judge a succession of persuasive voices, wrestling with what these encounters mean. We conclude with the catharsis of vicarious slaughter, the purging of untempered passion, and the promise of "peace and consolation." But Milton seems deliberately to leave readers of *Samson Agonistes* with as many questions as answers. What exactly has been won, and at what cost?

Samson Agonistes

Of that sort of Dramatic Poem which is called Tragedy

Tragedy, as it was anciently composed, hath been ever held the gravest, moralest, and most profitable of all other poems: therefore said by Aristotle to be of power by raising pity and fear, or terror, to purge the mind of those and such-like passions, that is to temper and reduce them to just measure with a kind of delight, stirred up by reading or seeing those passions well imitated.[1] Nor is nature wanting in her own effects to make good his assertion: for so in physic things of melancholic hue and quality are used against melancholy, sour against sour, salt to remove salt humours.[2] Hence philosophers and other gravest writers, as Cicero, Plutarch, and others, frequently cite out of tragic poets, both to adorn and illustrate their discourse. The Apostle Paul himself thought it not unworthy to insert a verse of Euripides[3] into the text of Holy Scripture, 1 Cor. 15.33, and

1 *Aristotle ... well imitated* Aristotle discusses tragic catharsis in *Poetics* 6.

2 *humours* The ancients ascribed four temperaments to excesses of one of the four humors (basic substances) believed to fill the human body: melancholic (black bile), choleric (yellow bile), phlegmatic (phlegm), and sanguine (blood).

3 *a verse of Euripides* "Evil communications corrupt good manners," a proverb usually now attributed to Menander rather than Euripides.

Paraeus[1] commenting on the Revelation, divides the whole book as a tragedy, into acts distinguished each by a chorus of heavenly harpings and song between. Heretofore men in highest dignity have laboured not a little to be thought able to compose a tragedy. Of that honour Dionysius the elder[2] was no less ambitious, than before of his attaining to the tyranny. Augustus Caesar[3] also had begun his *Ajax*, but unable to please his own judgment with what he had begun, left it unfinished. Seneca the philosopher[4] is by some thought the author of those tragedies (at least the best of them) that go under that name. Gregory Nazianzen,[5] a Father of the church, thought it not unbeseeming the sanctity of his person to write a tragedy, which he entitled *Christ Suffering*. This is mentioned to vindicate tragedy from the small esteem, or rather infamy, which in the account of many it undergoes at this day with other common interludes; happening through the poet's error of intermixing comic stuff with tragic sadness and gravity; or introducing trivial and vulgar persons, which by all judicious hath been counted absurd; and brought in without discretion, corruptly to gratify the people. And though ancient tragedy use no prologue, yet using sometimes, in case of self-defence, or explanation, that which Martial[6] calls an epistle; in behalf of this tragedy coming forth after the ancient manner, much different from what among us passes for best, thus much beforehand may be epistled: that chorus is here introduced after the Greek manner, not ancient only but modern, and still in use among the Italians. In the modelling therefore of this poem,

---

1 *Paraeus* David Paraeus (1548–1622), German Calvinist theologian and biblical commentator; his book on Revelation was published in 1618 and in English translation as *On the Divine Apocalypse* in 1644.

2 *Dionysius the elder* Dionysius I (c. 430–367 BCE), tyrant of Syracuse; he fancied himself a tragic poet.

3 *Augustus Caesar* Suetonius (born c. 69 CE) tells this story in his *Lives of the Caesars* 2.85.

4 *Seneca the philosopher* Lucius Annaeus Seneca (c. 4 BCE–65 CE) wrote philosophy (highly influential in the Renaissance) and drama, though his authorship of the tragedies remained under debate in the Renaissance.

5 *Gregory Nazianzen* Bishop of Constantinople (c. 329–89) and possible author of the play *Christus Patiens*.

6 *Martial* In the epistle to Book 2 of his *Epigrams*, the Latin poet Martial (c. 40–104 CE) noted that plays sometimes receive prologues because they "cannot speak for themselves" (that is, drama speaks in the voices of its characters whereas epigrams speak in the voice of the poet).

with good reason, the ancients and Italians are rather followed, as of much more authority and fame. The measure of verse used in the chorus is of all sorts, called by the Greeks monostrophic,[1] or rather apolelymenon,[2] without regard had to strophe, antistrophe, or epode, which were a kind of stanzas framed only for the music, then used with the chorus that sung; not essential to the poem, and therefore not material; or being divided into stanzas or pauses, they may be called alloeostropha.[3] Division into act and scene referring chiefly to the stage (to which this work never was intended) is here omitted.

It suffices if the whole drama be found not produced beyond the fifth act.[4] Of the style and uniformity, and that commonly called the plot, whether intricate or explicit,[5] which is nothing indeed but such economy, or disposition of the fable as may stand best with verisimilitude and decorum, they only will best judge who are not unacquainted with Aeschylus, Sophocles, and Euripides, the three tragic poets unequalled yet by any, and the best rule to all who endeavour to write tragedy. The circumscription of time wherein the whole drama begins and ends, is according to ancient rule,[6] and best example, within the space of twenty-four hours.

The Argument

Samson made captive, blind, and now in the prison at Gaza,[7] there to labour as in a common workhouse, on a festival day, in the general cessation from labour, comes forth into the open air, to a place

---

1 *monostrophic* Employing just one strophe or stanza, as opposed to the more usual arrangement in which speeches by the Chorus employed three stanzas: the strophe, antistrophe, and epode.

2 *apolelymenon* Greek: freed from strict stanzaic patterns.

3 *alloeostropha* Greek: of irregular strophes or stanzas.

4 *It suffices … fifth act* That is, while the poem lacks act and scene divisions, it still follows the traditional rules of drama by not extending its action past the concluding fifth-act catharsis.

5 *intricate or explicit* Complex or simple (alluding to Aristotle's discussion in *Poetics* 10).

6 *ancient rule* Aristotle observed in *Poetics* 5 that the action of tragedies generally took place within a span of twenty-four hours, but this unity of time only became a "rule" among Renaissance neo-classicists.

7 *Gaza* Then one of the main cities of the Philistines, Gaza has been inhabited since at least the 15th century BCE.

nigh, somewhat retired there to sit a while and bemoan his condition. Where he happens at length to be visited by certain friends and equals of his tribe, which make the Chorus, who seek to comfort him what they can; then by his old father Manoa, who endeavours the like, and withal tells him his purpose to procure his liberty by ransom; lastly, that this feast was proclaimed by the Philistines as a day of thanksgiving for their deliverance from the hands of Samson, which yet more troubles him. Manoa then departs to prosecute his endeavour with the Philistian lords for Samson's redemption; who in the meanwhile is visited by other persons; and lastly by a public officer to require his coming to the feast before the lords and people, to play or show his strength in their presence; he at first refuses, dismissing the public officer with absolute denial to come; at length persuaded inwardly that this was from God, he yields to go along with him, who came now the second time with great threatenings to fetch him; the Chorus yet remaining on the place, Manoa returns full of joyful hope, to procure ere long his son's deliverance: in the midst of which discourse an Hebrew comes in haste confusedly at first; and afterward more distinctly relating the catastrophe, what Samson had done to the Philistines, and by accident to himself; wherewith the tragedy ends.

The Persons

SAMSON
MANOA, the father of Samson
DALILA his wife
HARAPHA OF GATH
PUBLIC OFFICER
MESSENGER
CHORUS OF DANITES[1]

The Scene: before the prison in Gaza

SAMSON. A little onward lend thy guiding hand
To these dark steps, a little further on;

1 *DANITES* Members of the tribe to which Manoa and Samson belonged (see Judges 13.2).

For yonder bank hath choice of sun or shade,
There I am wont to sit, when any chance
Relieves me from my task of servile toil,
Daily in the common prison else enjoined me,
Where I a prisoner chained, scarce freely draw
The air imprisoned also, close and damp,
Unwholesome draught: but here I feel amends,
The breath of heaven fresh-blowing, pure and sweet,
With day-spring° born; here leave me to respire. *daybreak*
This day a solemn feast the people hold
To Dagon[1] their sea-idol, and forbid
Laborious works, unwillingly this rest
Their superstition yields me; hence with leave
Retiring from the popular noise, I seek
This unfrequented place to find some ease,
Ease to the body some, none to the mind
From restless thoughts, that like a deadly swarm
Of hornets armed, no sooner found alone,
But rush upon me thronging, and present
Times past, what once I was, and what am now.
O wherefore was my birth from heaven foretold
Twice by an angel, who at last in sight
Of both my parents all in flames ascended
From off the altar, where an offering burned,
As in a fiery column charioting
His godlike presence, and from some great act
Or benefit revealed to Abraham's race?[2]
Why was my breeding ordered and prescribed
As of a person separate to God,[3]
Designed for great exploits, if I must die
Betrayed, captived, and both my eyes put out,
Made of my enemies the scorn and gaze;

---

1 *Dagon* The Philistines' principal god, described in *Paradise Lost* as a "sea-monster, upward man / And downward fish" (1.462–63).

2 *O wherefore … race?* For the circumstances of Samson's birth, see Judges 13.3–5 and 10–23.

3 *separate to God* Samson is a Nazarite, a person set apart by ascetic vows to serve the divine: see Numbers 6.1–21 and Judges 13.4–7.

To grind in brazen fetters under task
With this heaven-gifted strength? O glorious strength
Put to the labour of a beast, debased
Lower than bond-slave! Promise was that I
Should Israel from Philistian yoke deliver;
Ask for this great deliverer now, and find him
Eyeless in Gaza at the mill with slaves,
Himself in bonds under Philistian yoke;
Yet stay, let me not rashly call in doubt
Divine prediction; what if all foretold
Had been fulfilled but through mine own default,
Whom have I to complain of but my self?
Who this high gift of strength committed to me,
In what part lodged, how easily bereft me,
Under the seal of silence could not keep,
But weakly to a woman must reveal it,
O'ercome with importunity and tears.
O impotence of mind, in body strong!
But what is strength without a double share
Of wisdom, vast, unwieldy, burdensome,
Proudly secure,° yet liable to fall *overconfident*
By weakest subtleties, not made to rule,
But to subserve where wisdom bears command.
God, when he gave me strength, to show withal
How slight the gift was, hung it in my hair.
But peace, I must not quarrel with the will
Of highest dispensation, which herein
Haply had ends above my reach to know:
Suffices that to me strength is my bane,
And proves the source of all my miseries;
So many, and so huge, that each apart
Would ask° a life to wail, but chief of all, *require*
O loss of sight, of thee I most complain!
Blind among enemies, O worse than chains,
Dungeon, or beggary, or decrepit age!
Light, the prime work of God, to me is extinct,
And all her various objects of delight
Annulled, which might in part my grief have eased,

Inferior to the vilest now become
Of man or worm; the vilest here excel me,
They creep, yet see, I dark in light exposed
To daily fraud, contempt, abuse and wrong,
Within doors, or without, still° as a fool, *always*
In power of others, never in my own;
Scarce half I seem to live, dead more than half.
O dark, dark, dark, amid the blaze of noon,
Irrecoverably dark, total eclipse
Without all hope of day!
O first-created beam, and thou great word,
Let there be light, and light was over all;
Why am I thus bereaved thy prime decree?
The sun to me is dark
And silent as the moon,
When she deserts the night
Hid in her vacant interlunar cave.[1]
Since light so necessary is to life,
And almost life itself, if it be true
That light is in the soul,
She all in every part; why was the sight
To such a tender ball as the eye confined?
So obvious° and so easy to be quenched, *vulnerable*
And not as feeling through all parts diffused,
That she might look at will through every pore?
Then had I not been thus exiled from light;
As in the land of darkness yet in light,
To live a life half dead, a living death,
And buried; but O yet more miserable!
My self, my sepulchre,° a moving grave, *tomb*
Buried, yet not exempt
By privilege of death and burial
From worst of other evils, pains and wrongs,
But made hereby obnoxious° more *exposed*
To all the miseries of life,

---

1 *silent as the moon ... interlunar cave* Silent in the sense of dark, vacant in the sense of idle or at leisure; in classical lore, the moon rested in a cave during the period of darkness between old and new moons.

Life in captivity
Among inhuman foes.
But who are these? For with joint pace I hear
The tread of many feet steering this way;
Perhaps my enemies who come to stare
At my affliction, and perhaps to insult,
Their daily practice to afflict me more.
Chorus. This, this is he; softly a while,
Let us not break in upon him;
O change beyond report, thought, or belief!
See how he lies at random, carelessly diffused,° *sprawled*
With languished head unpropped,
As one past hope, abandoned,
And by himself given over;
In slavish habit, ill-fitted weeds[1]
O'er-worn and soiled;
Or do my eyes misrepresent? Can this be he,
That heroic, that renowned,
Irresistible Samson? Whom unarmed
No strength of man, or fiercest wild beast could withstand;
Who tore the lion, as the lion tears the kid,
Ran on embattled armies clad in iron,
And weaponless himself,
Made arms ridiculous, useless the forgery° *manufacture*
Of brazen shield and spear, the hammered cuirass,° *breastplate*
Chalybean tempered steel,[2] and frock of mail
Adamantean proof;[3]
But safest he who stood aloof,
When insupportably[4] his foot advanced,
In scorn of their proud arms and warlike tools,
Spurned them to death by troops. The bold Ascalonite[5]

---

1 *slavish habit, ill-fitted weeds* Attired in clothing suitable for slave laborers.

2 *Chalybean tempered steel* The Chalybes were a Black Sea tribe famous in the classical period for their work in iron and steel.

3 *Adamantean proof* Capable of resisting adamant, a fabled mineral hard as diamond.

4 *insupportably his foot advanced* He was drawn forward irresistably.

5 *Ascalonite* Ascalon was a Philistine city.

Fled from his lion ramp,° old warriors turned *lion-like spring*
Their plated backs under his heel;
Or grovelling soiled their crested helmets in the dust.
Then with what trivial weapon came to hand,
The jaw of a dead ass, his sword of bone,
A thousand foreskins[1] fell, the flower of Palestine[2]
In Ramath-lechi[3] famous to this day:
Then by main force pulled up, and on his shoulders bore
The gates of Azza,° post, and massy bar *Gaza (variant form)*
Up to the hill by Hebron, seat of giants old,[4]
No journey of a Sabbath day,[5] and loaded so;
Like whom the Gentiles feign to bear up heaven.[6]
Which shall I first bewail,
Thy bondage or lost sight,
Prison within prison
Inseparably dark?
Thou art become (O worst imprisonment!)
The dungeon of thy self; thy soul
(Which men enjoying sight oft without cause complain)
Imprisoned now indeed,
In real darkness of the body dwells,
Shut up from outward light
To incorporate with gloomy night;
For inward light alas
Puts forth no visual beam.
O mirror of our fickle state,
Since man on earth unparalleled!
The rarer thy example stands,
By how much from the top of wondrous glory,
Strongest of mortal men,

---

1 *foreskins* Synecdoche for the uncircumcised Philistines.

2 *Palestine* The territory of the Philistines.

3 *Ramath-lechi* "Jawbone Height," a hill on the frontier between Judah and Palestine.

4 *Hebron … giants old* Hebron was originally a Canaanite royal city, approximately 40 miles from Gaza. Numbers 13.22–33 talks about the giants of Hebron.

5 *No journey of a Sabbath day* The Chorus indulges in epic understatement: Jewish law restricted travel on the Sabbath to about a mile (give or take a half-mile); Samson carried the heavy city gates about forty miles.

6 *whom the Gentiles … bear up heaven* Atlas, one of the Titans in Greek myth.

To lowest pitch of abject fortune thou art fallen.
For him I reckon not in high estate
Whom long descent of birth
Or the sphere of fortune[1] raises;
But thee whose strength, while virtue was her mate,
Might have subdued the earth,
Universally crowned with highest praises.

SAMSON. I hear the sound of words, their sense the air
Dissolves unjointed ere it reach my ear.

CHORUS. He speaks, let us draw nigh. Matchless in might,
The glory late of Israel, now the grief;
We come thy friends and neighbours not unknown
From Eshtaol and Zora's[2] fruitful vale
To visit or bewail thee, or if better,
Counsel or consolation we may bring,
Salve to thy sores; apt words have power to swage° *assuage*
The tumours of a troubled mind,
And are as balm to festered wounds.

SAMSON. Your coming, friends, revives me, for I learn
Now of my own experience, not by talk,
How counterfeit a coin they are who friends
Bear in their superscription[3] (of the most
I would be understood): in prosperous days
They swarm, but in adverse withdraw their head
Not to be found, though sought. Ye see, O friends,
How many evils have enclosed me round;
Yet that which was the worst now least afflicts me,
Blindness, for had I sight, confused with shame,
How could I once look up, or heave the head,
Who like a foolish pilot have shipwrecked
My vessel trusted to me from above,
Gloriously rigged; and for a word, a tear,
Fool, have divulged the secret gift of God
To a deceitful woman: tell me friends,
Am I not sung and proverbed for a fool

---

1 *sphere of fortune* Wheel of fortune.
2 *Eshtaol and Zora* Two towns of the tribe of Dan.
3 *superscription* Words or value inscribed on a coin.

In every street, do they not say, how well
Are come upon him his deserts? Yet why?
Immeasurable strength they might behold
In me, of wisdom nothing more than mean;° *average*
This with the other should, at least, have paired,
These two proportioned ill drove me transverse.° *off course*
Chorus. Tax° not divine disposal, wisest men *accuse, blame*
Have erred, and by bad women been deceived;
And shall again, pretend they ne'er so wise.
Deject not then so overmuch thy self,
Who hast of sorrow thy full load besides;
Yet truth to say, I oft have heard men wonder
Why thou shouldst wed Philistian women rather
Than of thine own tribe fairer, or as fair,
At least of thy own nation, and as noble.
Samson. The first I saw at Timna,[1] and she pleased
Me, not my parents, that I sought to wed,
The daughter of an infidel: they knew not
That what I motioned° was of God; I knew *signalled*
From intimate impulse, and therefore urged
The marriage on; that by occasion hence
I might begin Israel's deliverance,
The work to which I was divinely called;
She proving false, the next I took to wife
(O that I never had! fond wish too late)
Was in the vale of Sorec, Dalila,
That specious monster, my accomplished snare.
I thought it lawful from my former act,
And the same end; still watching to oppress
Israel's oppressors: of what now I suffer
She was not the prime cause, but I my self,
Who vanquished with a peal of words (O weakness!)
Gave up my fort of silence to a woman.
Chorus. In seeking just occasion to provoke
The Philistine, thy country's enemy,
Thou never wast remiss, I bear thee witness:
Yet Israel still serves with all his sons.

1 *Timna* Philistine city in Canaan.

SAMSON. That fault I take not on me, but transfer
On Israel's governors, and heads of tribes,
Who seeing those great acts which God had done
Singly by me against their conquerors
Acknowledged not, or not at all considered
Deliverance offered: I on the other side
Used no ambition to commend my deeds,
The deeds themselves, though mute, spoke loud the doer;
But they persisted deaf, and would not seem
To count them things worth notice, till at length
Their lords the Philistines with gathered powers
Entered Judea seeking me, who then
Safe to the rock of Etham[1] was retired,
Not flying, but forecasting in what place
To set upon them, what advantaged best;
Meanwhile the men of Judah to prevent
The harass of their land, beset me round;
I willingly on some conditions came
Into their hands, and they as gladly yield me
To the uncircumcised a welcome prey,
Bound with two cords; but cords to me were threads
Touched with the flame: on their whole host I flew
Unarmed, and with a trivial weapon felled
Their choicest youth; they only lived who fled.
Had Judah that day joined, or one whole tribe,
They had by this possessed the towers of Gath,[2]
And lorded over them whom now they serve;
But what more oft in nations grown corrupt,
And by their vices brought to servitude,
Than to love bondage more than liberty,
Bondage with ease than strenuous liberty;
And to despise, or envy, or suspect
Whom God hath of his special favour raised
As their deliverer; if he aught begin,
How frequent to desert him, and at last
To heap ingratitude on worthiest deeds?

---

1 *Etham* On the road between Hebron and Jerusalem.

2 *Gath* One of the five Philistine city-states.

Chorus. Thy words to my remembrance bring
How Succoth and the fort of Penuel
Their great deliverer contemned,[1]
The matchless Gideon[2] in pursuit
Of Madian and her vanquished kings:
And how ingrateful Ephraim[3]
Had dealt with Jephtha, who by argument,
Not worse than by his shield and spear
Defended Israel from the Ammonite,
Had not his prowess quelled their pride
In that sore battle when so many died
Without reprieve adjudged to death,
For want of well pronouncing *shibboleth*.
Samson. Of such examples add me to the roll;
Me easily indeed mine may neglect,
But God's proposed deliverance not so.
Chorus. Just are the ways of God,
And justifiable to men;
Unless there be who think not God at all,
If any be, they walk obscure;° — *in darkness*
For of such doctrine never was there school,
But the heart of the fool,[4]
And no man therein doctor° but himself. — *teacher*
Yet more there be who doubt his ways not just,
As to his own edicts, found contradicting,
Then give the reins to wandering thought,
Regardless of his glory's diminution;
Till by their own perplexities involved
They ravel° more, still° less resolved, — *tangle / always*

---

1 *contemned* Treated with contempt.

2 *Gideon* See Judges 8.4–9; the Israelites in Succoth and Penuel refused to provide Gideon and his army with supplies as they pursued the remaining leaders of a recently defeated Midian (here, Madian) force.

3 *Ephraim* See Judges 11.12–33, 12.1–6; after the men of Ephraim refused to help Jephtha fight the Ammonites, Jephtha slaughtered them in retribution; his men afterward identified any Ephraimite fugitives by their distinctive pronunciation of the Hebrew word "shibboleth" (meaning an ear of grain).

4 *the heart of the fool* "The fool hath said in his heart, There is no God" (Psalms 14.1).

But never find self-satisfying solution.
As if they would confine the interminable,
And tie him to his own prescript,
Who made our laws to bind us, not himself,
And hath full right to exempt
Whom so it pleases him by choice
From national obstriction,[1] without taint
Of sin, or legal debt;
For with his own laws he can best dispense.
He would not else who never wanted means,
Nor in respect of the enemy just cause
To set his people free,
Have prompted this heroic Nazarite,
Against his vow of strictest purity,
To seek in marriage that fallacious bride,
Unclean, unchaste.
Down Reason then, at least vain reasonings down,
Though Reason here aver° *assert*
That moral verdict quits her of unclean:
Unchaste was subsequent,[2] her stain not his.
But see here comes thy reverend sire
With careful° step, locks white as down, *anxious*
Old Manoa: advise
Forthwith how thou ought'st to receive him.
Samson. Ay me, another inward grief awaked,
With mention of that name renews the assault.
Manoa. Brethren and men of Dan,[3] for such ye seem,
Though in this uncouth° place; if old respect, *unfamiliar*
As I suppose, towards your once gloried friend,
My son now captive, hither hath informed° *guided*
Your younger feet, while mine cast back with age
Came lagging after; say if he be here.
Chorus. As signal° now in low dejected state, *outstanding*
As erst° in highest, behold him where he lies. *formerly*

---

1 *obstriction* Legal obligation, in this case not to marry a Gentile (Deuteronomy 7.3).

2 *Unchaste was subsequent* See Judges 14.20; Samson's first wife, the woman of Timna, was given to his companion after Samson rejected her.

3 *men of Dan* Danites.

MANOA. O miserable change! Is this the man,
That invincible Samson, far renowned,
The dread of Israel's foes, who with a strength
Equivalent to angels walked their streets,
None offering fight; who single combatant
Duelled their armies ranked in proud array,
Himself an army, now unequal match
To save himself against a coward armed
At one spear's length. O ever-failing trust
In mortal strength! and O what not in man
Deceivable and vain! Nay what thing good
Prayed for, but often proves our woe, our bane?
I prayed for children, and thought barrenness
In wedlock a reproach; I gained a son,
And such a son as all men hailed me happy;
Who would be now a father in my stead?
O wherefore did God grant me my request,
And as a blessing with such pomp adorned?
Why are his gifts desirable, to tempt
Our earnest prayers, then given with solemn hand
As graces, draw a scorpion's tail behind?
For this did the angel twice descend? For this
Ordained thy nurture holy, as of a plant;
Select, and sacred, glorious for a while,
The miracle of men: then in an hour
Ensnared, assaulted, overcome, led bound,
Thy foes' derision, captive, poor, and blind
Into a dungeon thrust, to work with slaves?
Alas methinks whom God hath chosen once
To worthiest deeds, if he through frailty err,
He should not so o'erwhelm, and as a thrall
Subject him to so foul indignities,
Be it but for honour's sake of former deeds.
SAMSON. Appoint[1] not heavenly disposition, father,
Nothing of all these evils hath befall'n me
But justly; I my self have brought them on,

1 *Appoint* Both blame, and limit or prescribe.

Sole author I, sole cause: if aught seem vile,
As vile hath been my folly, who have profaned
The mystery of God given me under pledge
Of vow, and have betrayed it to a woman,
A Canaanite, my faithless enemy.
This well I knew, nor was at all surprised,
But warned by oft experience: did not she
Of Timna first betray me, and reveal
The secret wrested from me in her highth° *height*
Of nuptial love professed, carrying it straight
To them who had corrupted her, my spies,
And rivals? In this other was there found
More faith? Who also in her prime of love,
Spousal embraces, vitiated° with gold, *corrupted*
Though offered only, by the scent[1] conceived
Her spurious first-born, treason against me?
Thrice she assayed° with flattering prayers and sighs, *attempted*
And amorous reproaches to win from me
My capital[2] secret, in what part my strength
Lay stored, in what part summed, that she might know:
Thrice I deluded her, and turned to sport
Her importunity, each time perceiving
How openly, and with what impudence
She purposed to betray me, and (which was worse
Than undissembled hate) with what contempt
She sought to make me traitor to my self;
Yet the fourth time, when mustering all her wiles,
With blandished parleys, feminine assaults,
Tongue-batteries, she surceased not day nor night
To storm me over-watched, and wearied out.
At times when men seek most repose and rest,
I yielded, and unlocked her all my heart,
Who with a grain of manhood well resolved
Might easily have shook off all her snares:
But foul effeminacy held me yoked

1 *by the scent* Through the sense or perception of the offered bribe.

2 *capital* Pun: not only his most important and furthermore lethal secret, but a secret pertaining to his head ("capital" derives from the Latin for "head").

Her bond-slave; O indignity, O blot
To honour and religion! servile mind
Rewarded well with servile punishment!
The base degree to which I now am fall'n,
These rags, this grinding, is not yet so base
As was my former servitude, ignoble,
Unmanly, ignominious, infamous,
True slavery, and that blindness worse than this,
That saw not how degenerately I served.
Manoa. I cannot praise thy marriage choices, son,
Rather approved them not; but thou didst plead
Divine impulsion prompting how thou might'st
Find some occasion to infest° our foes. *harass*
I state not that; this I am sure; our foes
Found soon occasion thereby to make thee
Their captive, and their triumph; thou the sooner
Temptation found'st, or over-potent charms
To violate the sacred trust of silence
Deposited within thee; which to have kept
Tacit,° was in thy power. True; and thou bear'st *implicit*
Enough, and more the burden of that fault;
Bitterly hast thou paid, and still art paying
That rigid score.° A worse thing yet remains, *debt*
This day the Philistines a popular feast
Here celebrate in Gaza, and proclaim
Great pomp, and sacrifice, and praises loud
To Dagon, as their god who hath delivered
Thee Samson bound and blind into their hands,
Them out of thine, who slew'st them many a slain.
So Dagon shall be magnified, and God,
Besides whom is no god, compared with idols,
Disglorified, blasphemed, and had in scorn
By the idolatrous rout amidst their wine;
Which to have come to pass by means of thee,
Samson, of all thy sufferings think the heaviest,
Of all reproach the most with shame that ever
Could have befall'n thee and thy father's house.
Samson. Father, I do acknowledge and confess
That I this honour, I this pomp have brought

To Dagon, and advanced his praises high
Among the heathen round; to God have brought
Dishonour, obloquy,° and oped the mouths *condemnation*
Of idolists, and atheists; have brought scandal
To Israel, diffidence° of God, and doubt *distrust*
In feeble hearts, propense° enough before *disposed*
To waver, or fall off and join with idols;
Which is my chief affliction, shame and sorrow,
The anguish of my soul, that suffers not
Mine eye to harbour sleep, or thoughts to rest.
This only hope relieves me, that the strife
With me hath end; all the contest is now
'Twixt God and Dagon; Dagon hath presumed,
Me overthrown, to enter lists[1] with God,
His deity comparing and preferring
Before the God of Abraham. He, be sure,
Will not connive,° or linger, thus provoked, *be tolerant*
But will arise and his great name assert:
Dagon must stoop, and shall ere long receive
Such a discomfit, as shall quite despoil him
Of all these boasted trophies won on me,
And with confusion blank his worshippers.
MANOA. With cause this hope relieves thee, and these words
I as a prophecy receive: for God,
Nothing more certain, will not long defer
To vindicate the glory of his name
Against all competition, nor will long
Endure it, doubtful whether God be Lord,
Or Dagon. But for thee what shall be done?
Thou must not in the meanwhile here forgot
Lie in this miserable loathsome plight
Neglected. I already have made way
To some Philistian lords, with whom to treat
About thy ransom: well they may by this
Have satisfied their utmost of revenge
By pains and slaveries, worse than death inflicted
On thee, who now no more canst do them harm.

1 *to enter lists* To enter jousting grounds.

SAMSON. Spare that proposal, father, spare the trouble
Of that solicitation; let me here,
As I deserve, pay on my punishment;
And expiate, if possible, my crime,
Shameful garrulity.[1] To have revealed
Secrets of men, the secrets of a friend,
How heinous had the fact been, how deserving
Contempt, and scorn of all, to be excluded
All friendship, and avoided as a blab,
The mark of fool set on his front! But I
God's counsel have not kept, his holy secret
Presumptuously have published, impiously,
Weakly at least, and shamefully: a sin
That Gentiles in their parables condemn
To their abyss and horrid pains confined.
MANOA. Be penitent and for thy fault contrite,
But act not in thy own affliction, son,
Repent the sin, but if the punishment
Thou canst avoid, self-preservation bids;
Or the execution leave to high disposal,
And let another hand, not thine, exact
Thy penal forfeit from thy self; perhaps
God will relent, and quit thee all his debt;
Who evermore approves and more accepts
(Best pleased with humble and filial submission)
Him who imploring mercy sues for life,
Than who self-rigorous chooses death as due;
Which argues over-just, and self-displeased
For self-offence, more than for God offended.
Reject not then what offered means, who knows
But God hath set before us, to return thee
Home to thy country and his sacred house,
Where thou may'st bring thy off'rings, to avert
His further ire, with prayers and vows renewed.

---

1 *Shameful garrulity* Milton's use of the phrase may be an allusion to Ovid's description of the crime of Tantalus, as mentioned in *The Art of Love*, 2.606: *Garrulus in media Tantalus aret aqua* (His garrulous tongue left dry Tantalus searching for water).

SAMSON. His pardon I implore; but as for life,
To what end should I seek it? When in strength
All mortals I excelled, and great in hopes
With youthful courage and magnanimous thoughts
Of birth from heaven foretold and high exploits,
Full of divine instinct, after some proof
Of acts indeed heroic, far beyond
The sons of Anak,[1] famous now and blazed,
Fearless of danger, like a petty god
I walked about admired of all and dreaded
On hostile ground, none daring my affront.[2]
Then swoll'n with pride into the snare I fell
Of fair fallacious looks, venereal trains,[3]
Softened with pleasure and voluptuous life;
At length to lay my head and hallowed pledge
Of all my strength in the lascivious lap
Of a deceitful concubine who shore me
Like a tame wether,[4] all my precious fleece,
Then turned me out ridiculous, despoiled,
Shaven, and disarmed among my enemies.
CHORUS. Desire of wine and all delicious drinks,
Which many a famous warrior overturns,
Thou couldst repress, nor did the dancing ruby
Sparkling, out-poured, the flavour, or the smell,
Or taste that cheers the heart of gods and men,
Allure thee from the cool crystalline stream.[5]
SAMSON. Wherever fountain or fresh current flowed
Against° the eastern ray, translucent, pure *towards*
With touch ethereal of heaven's fiery rod° *sunray*
I drank, from the clear milky juice[6] allaying

---

1 *sons of Anak* Giants (from Numbers 13.33).

2 *none daring my affront* None daring to encounter or offend me.

3 *venereal trains* Snares of Venus.

4 *wether* Castrated ram.

5 *Desire of wine … stream* As a Nazarite, Samson had taken a vow to abstain from alcohol (Judges 13.4).

6 *clear milky juice* Clear, pure water. Milton also describes water from a stream as "milky" in *Paradise Lost* 5.306. The usage suggests the conception of the earth as mother.

Thirst, and refreshed; nor envied them the grape
Whose heads that turbulent liquor fills with fumes.
Chorus. O madness, to think use of strongest wines
And strongest drinks our chief support of health,
When God with these forbidden made choice to rear
His mighty champion, strong above compare,
Whose drink was only from the liquid brook.
Samson. But what availed this temperance, not complete
Against another object more enticing?
What boots° it at one gate to make defence, *profits*
And at another to let in the foe,
Effeminately vanquished? By which means,
Now blind, disheartened, shamed, dishonoured, quelled,
To what can I be useful, wherein serve
My nation, and the work from heaven imposed,
But to sit idle on the household hearth,
A burdenous drone; to visitants a gaze,
Or pitied object, these redundant° locks *abundant*
Robustious° to no purpose clustering down, *robust, strong*
Vain monument of strength; till length of years
And sedentary numbness craze° my limbs *disable*
To a contemptible old age obscure.
Here rather let me drudge and earn my bread,
Till vermin or the draff° of servile food *dregs*
Consume me, and oft-invocated death
Hasten the welcome end of all my pains.
Manoa. Wilt thou then serve the Philistines with that gift
Which was expressly given thee to annoy° them? *harm*
Better at home lie bed-rid, not only idle,
Inglorious, unemployed, with age outworn.
But God who caused a fountain at thy prayer
From the dry ground to spring, thy thirst to allay
After the brunt of battle, can as easy
Cause light again within thy eyes to spring,
Wherewith to serve him better than thou hast;
And I persuade me so; why else this strength
Miraculous yet remaining in those locks?
His might continues in thee not for naught,

Nor shall his wondrous gifts be frustrate thus.
Samson. All otherwise to me my thoughts portend,
That these dark orbs no more shall treat with light,
Nor the other light of life continue long,
But yield to double darkness nigh at hand:
So much I feel my genial spirits[1] droop,
My hopes all flat, nature within me seems
In all her functions weary of herself;
My race of glory run, and race of shame,
And I shall shortly be with them that rest.
Manoa. Believe not these suggestions which proceed
From anguish of the mind and humours black,[2]
That mingle with thy fancy. I however
Must not omit a father's timely care
To prosecute the means of thy deliverance
By ransom or how else: meanwhile be calm,
And healing words from these thy friends admit.
Samson. O that torment should not be confined
To the body's wounds and sores
With maladies innumerable
In heart, head, breast, and reins;° *kidneys*
But must secret passage find
To the inmost mind,
There exercise all his fierce accidents,° *symptoms*
And on her purest spirits prey,
As on entrails, joints, and limbs,
With answerable pains, but more intense,
Though void of corporal sense.
My griefs not only pain me
As a lingering disease,
But finding no redress, ferment and rage,
Nor less than wounds immedicable° *incurable*
Rankle, and fester, and gangrene,
To black mortification.
Thoughts my tormentors armed with deadly stings

---

1 *genial spirits* Spirits underlying one's nature.

2 *humours black* Black bile, one of the four humors of Renaissance medical psychology and thought to produce melancholy.

Mangle my apprehensive° tenderest parts, *sensitive*
Exasperate, exulcerate, and raise
Dire inflammation which no cooling herb
Or med'cinal liquor can assuage,
Nor breath of vernal air from snowy alp.
Sleep hath forsook and given me o'er
To death's benumbing opium as my only cure.
Thence faintings, swoonings of despair,
And sense of heaven's desertion.
        I was his nursling once and choice delight,
His destined from the womb,
Promised by heavenly message twice descending.
Under his special eye
Abstemious I grew up and thrived amain;° *mightily*
He led me on to mightiest deeds
Above the nerve of mortal arm
Against the uncircumcised, our enemies.
But now hath cast me off as never known,
And to those cruel enemies,
Whom I by his appointment had provoked,
Left me all helpless with the irreparable loss
Of sight, reserved alive to be repeated
The subject of their cruelty, or scorn.
Nor am I in the list of them that hope;
Hopeless are all my evils, all remediless;
This one prayer yet remains, might I be heard,
No long petition, speedy death,
The close of all my miseries, and the balm.
Chorus. Many are the sayings of the wise
In ancient and in modern books enrolled;[1]
Extolling patience as the truest fortitude;[2]
And to the bearing well of all calamities,
All chances incident to man's frail life
Consolatories writ
With studied argument, and much persuasion sought

---

1 *enrolled* Ancient books were found in scrolls (rolls).

2 *patience as the truest fortitude* Milton himself expressed this "wise" saying in a "modern book": see *Paradise Lost* 9.31–33 and 12.569–70.

Lenient of grief and anxious thought,
But with the afflicted in his pangs their sound
Little prevails, or rather seems a tune,
Harsh, and of dissonant mood from his complaint,
Unless he feel within
Some source of consolation from above;
Secret refreshings, that repair his strength,
And fainting spirits uphold.
God of our fathers, what is man!
That thou towards him with hand so various,
Or might I say contrarious,
Temper'st thy providence[1] through his short course,
Not evenly, as thou rul'st
The angelic orders and inferior creatures mute,
Irrational and brute.
Nor do I name of men the common rout,
That wand'ring loose about
Grow up and perish, as the summer fly,
Heads without name no more remembered,
But such as thou hast solemnly elected,
With gifts and graces eminently adorned
To some great work, thy glory,
And people's safety, which in part they effect:
Yet toward these thus dignified, thou oft
Amidst their height of noon,
Changest thy countenance, and thy hand with no regard
Of highest favours past
From thee on them, or them to thee of service.
Nor only dost degrade them, or remit
To life obscured, which were a fair dismission,° *dismissal*
But throw'st them lower than thou didst exalt them high,
Unseemly falls in human eye,
Too grievous for the trespass or omission,
Oft leav'st them to the hostile sword
Of heathen and profane, their carcasses
To dogs and fowls a prey, or else captived:

1 *Temper'st thy providence* Neutralizes or counterbalances [God's] protective care.

Or to the unjust tribunals, under change of times,
And condemnation of the ingrateful multitude.[1]
If these they scape, perhaps in poverty
With sickness and disease thou bow'st them down,
Painful diseases and deformed,
In crude° old age; *premature*
Though not disordinate,° yet causeless suffering *intemperate*
The punishment of dissolute days, in fine,
Just or unjust, alike seem miserable,
For oft alike, both come to evil end.
        So deal not with this once thy glorious champion,
The image of thy strength, and mighty minister.
What do I beg? How hast thou dealt already?
Behold him in this state calamitous, and turn
His labours, for thou canst, to peaceful end.
        But who is this, what thing of sea or land?
Female of sex it seems,
That so bedecked, ornate, and gay,
Comes this way sailing
Like a stately ship
Of Tarsus, bound for th' isles
Of Javan or Gadier[2]
With all her bravery° on, and tackle trim, *finery*
Sails filled, and streamers waving,
Courted by all the winds that hold them play,
An amber scent[3] of odorous perfume
Her harbinger, a damsel train behind;
Some rich Philistian matron she may seem,
And now at nearer view, no other certain

---

1 *their carcasses ... ingrateful multitude* This passage partly echoes Homer's description of those who died in the Trojan war (*Iliad* 1.4–5). Most readers also hear an allusion to the fates of parliamentary leaders at the Restoration: those who remained alive were tried and several imprisoned or executed, and the bodies of some deceased regicides were exhumed and displayed to the public.

2 *Tarsus* The location of the biblical Tarshish is disputed, but Milton appears to side with those who place it in Cicilia (modern-day Turkey), cf. *Paradise Lost* 1.200; *Javan* Greek islands (cf. *Paradise Lost* 1.508); *Gadier* Cadiz.

3 *amber scent* Ambergris is a waxy substance secreted by sperm whales and used in the manufacture of perfume as a fixative, now illegal in many countries.

Than Dalila thy wife.

SAMSON. My wife, my traitress, let her not come near me.

CHORUS. Yet on she moves, now stands and eyes thee fixed,
About t' have spoke, but now, with head declined
Like a fair flower surcharged with dew, she weeps
And words addressed seem into tears dissolved,
Wetting the borders of her silken veil:
But now again she makes address° to speak. *preparation*

DALILA. With doubtful feet and wavering resolution
I came, still dreading thy displeasure, Samson,
Which to have merited, without excuse,
I cannot but acknowledge; yet if tears
May expiate (though the fact more evil drew
In the perverse event than I foresaw)
My penance hath not slackened, though my pardon
No way assured. But conjugal affection
Prevailing over fear, and timorous doubt
Hath led me on desirous to behold
Once more thy face, and know of thy estate.° *condition*
If aught in my ability may serve
To lighten what thou suffer'st, and appease
Thy mind with what amends is in my power,
Though late, yet in some part to recompense
My rash but more unfortunate misdeed.

SAMSON. Out, out hyena;[1] these are thy wonted° arts, *habitual*
And arts of every woman false like thee,
To break all faith, all vows, deceive, betray,
Then as repentant to submit, beseech,
And reconcilement move with feigned remorse,
Confess, and promise wonders in her change,
Not truly penitent, but chief to try
Her husband, how far urged his patience bears,
His virtue or weakness which way to assail:
Then with more cautious and instructed skill
Again transgresses, and again submits;

---

1 *hyena* According to Pliny the Elder (23-79 CE), the hyena can imitate the human voice: "among the shepherds' homesteads it simulates human speech, and picks up the name of one of them so as to call him to come out of doors and tear him in pieces."

That wisest and best men full oft beguiled
With goodness principled[1] not to reject
The penitent, but ever to forgive,
Are drawn to wear out miserable days,
Entangled with a poisonous bosom snake,
If not by quick destruction soon cut off
As I by thee, to ages an example.
Dalila. Yet hear me Samson; not that I endeavour
To lessen or extenuate my offence,
But that on the other side, if it be weighed
By itself, with aggravations not surcharged,
Or else with just allowance counterpoised,
I may, if possible, thy pardon find
The easier towards me, or thy hatred less.
First granting, as I do, it was a weakness
In me, but incident to all our sex,
Curiosity, inquisitive, importune
Of secrets, then with like infirmity
To publish them, both common female faults:
Was it not weakness also to make known
For importunity, that is for naught,
Wherein consisted all thy strength and safety?
To what I did thou show'dst me first the way.
But I to enemies revealed, and should not.
Nor shouldst thou have trusted that to woman's frailty:
Ere I to thee, thou to thy self wast cruel.
Let weakness then with weakness come to parle° *parley*
So near related, or the same of kind,
Thine forgive mine; that men may censure thine
The gentler, if severely thou exact not
More strength from me, than in thy self was found.
And what if love, which thou interpret'st hate,
The jealousy of love, powerful of sway
In human hearts, nor less in mine towards thee,
Caused what I did? I saw thee mutable

1 *principled* Instructed, in order to demonstrate one's adherence to one's principles.

Of fancy,[1] feared lest one day thou wouldst leave me
As her at Timna, sought by all means therefore
How to endear, and hold thee to me firmest:
No better way I saw than by importuning
To learn thy secrets, get into my power
Thy key of strength and safety: thou wilt say,
Why then revealed? I was assured by those
Who tempted me, that nothing was designed
Against thee but safe custody, and hold:
That made for me; I knew that liberty
Would draw thee forth to perilous enterprises,
While I at home sat full of cares and fears
Wailing thy absence in my widowed bed;
Here I should still enjoy thee day and night
Mine and love's prisoner, not the Philistines',
Whole to myself, unhazarded abroad,
Fearless at home of partners in my love.
These reasons in love's law have passed for good,
Though fond° and reasonless to some perhaps; *foolish*
And love hath oft, well meaning, wrought much woe,
Yet always pity or pardon hath obtained.
Be not unlike all others, not austere
As thou art strong, inflexible as steel.
If thou in strength all mortals dost exceed,
In uncompassionate anger do not so.

SAMSON. How cunningly the sorceress displays
Her own transgressions, to upbraid me mine!
That malice not repentance brought thee hither,
By this appears: I gave, thou say'st, the example,
I led the way; bitter reproach, but true,
I to myself was false ere thou to me,
Such pardon therefore as I give my folly,
Take to thy wicked deed: which when thou seest
Impartial, self-severe, inexorable,
Thou wilt renounce thy seeking, and much rather
Confess it feigned, weakness is thy excuse,

1 *mutable of fancy* Liable to change one's affections.

And I believe it, weakness to resist
Philistian gold: if weakness may excuse,
What murderer, what traitor, parricide,
Incestuous, sacrilegious, but may plead it?
All wickedness is weakness: that plea therefore
With God or man will gain thee no remission.
But love constrained thee; call it furious rage
To satisfy thy lust: love seeks to have love;
My love how couldst thou hope, who took'st the way
To raise in me inexpiable hate,
Knowing, as needs I must, by thee betrayed?
In vain thou striv'st to cover shame with shame,
Or by evasions thy crime uncover'st more.

DALILA. Since thou determin'st weakness for no plea
In man or woman, though to thy own condemning,
Hear what assaults I had, what snares besides,
What sieges girt° me round, ere I consented; *encircled*
Which might have awed the best-resolved of men,
The constantest to have yielded without blame.
It was not gold, as to my charge thou lay'st,
That wrought with me: thou know'st the magistrates
And princes of my country came in person,
Solicited, commanded, threatened, urged,
Adjured by all the bonds of civil duty
And of religion, pressed how just it was,
How honourable, how glorious to entrap
A common enemy, who had destroyed
Such numbers of our nation: and the priest[1]
Was not behind, but ever at my ear,
Preaching how meritorious with the gods
It would be to ensnare an irreligious
Dishonourer of Dagon: what had I
To oppose against such powerful arguments?
Only my love of thee held long debate;
And combated in silence all these reasons
With hard contest: at length that grounded maxim

1 *priest* One of Milton's additions to the biblical account.

So rife and celebrated in the mouths
Of wisest men; that to the public good
Private respects must yield; with grave authority
Took full possession of me and prevailed;
Virtue, as I thought, truth, duty so enjoining.

Samson. I thought where all thy circling wiles would end;
In feigned religion, smooth hypocrisy.
But had thy love, still odiously pretended,
Been, as it ought, sincere, it would have taught thee
Far other reasonings, brought forth other deeds.
I before all the daughters of my tribe
And of my nation chose thee from among
My enemies, loved thee, as too well thou knew'st,
Too well, unbosomed all my secrets to thee,
Not out of levity, but overpowered
By thy request, who could deny thee nothing;
Yet now am judged an enemy. Why then
Didst thou at first receive me for thy husband?
Then, as since then, thy country's foe professed:
Being once a wife, for me thou wast to leave
Parents and country; nor was I their subject,
Nor under their protection but my own,
Thou mine, not theirs: if aught against my life
Thy country sought of thee, it sought unjustly,
Against the law of nature, law of nations,
No more thy country, but an impious crew
Of men conspiring to uphold their state
By worse than hostile deeds, violating the ends
For which our country is a name so dear;
Not therefore to be obeyed. But zeal moved thee;
To please thy gods thou didst it; gods unable
To acquit° themselves and prosecute their foes *vindicate*
But by ungodly deeds, the contradiction
Of their own deity, gods cannot be:
Less therefore to be pleased, obeyed, or feared,
These false pretexts and varnished colours failing,
Bare in thy guilt how foul must thou appear!

DALILA. In argument with men a woman ever
Goes by the worse, whatever be her cause.
SAMSON. For want of words no doubt, or lack of breath,
Witness when I was worried with thy peals.
DALILA. I was a fool, too rash, and quite mistaken
In what I thought would have succeeded best.
Let me obtain forgiveness of thee, Samson,
Afford me place° to show what recompense *opportunity*
Towards thee I intend for what I have misdone,
Misguided; only what remains past cure
Bear not too sensibly,° nor still insist *keenly*
To afflict thy self in vain: though sight be lost,
Life yet hath many solaces, enjoyed
Where other senses want not their delights
At home in leisure and domestic ease,
Exempt from many a care and chance to which
Eyesight exposes daily men abroad.° *outdoors*
I to the lords will intercede, not doubting
Their favourable ear, that I may fetch thee
From forth this loathsome prison-house, to abide
With me, where my redoubled love and care
With nursing diligence, to me glad office,
May ever tend about thee to old age
With all things grateful cheered, and so supplied,
That what by me thou hast lost thou least shalt miss.
SAMSON. No, no, of my condition take no care;
It fits not; thou and I long since are twain;
Nor think me so unwary or accursed
To bring my feet again into the snare
Where once I have been caught; I know thy trains
Though dearly to my cost, thy gins, and toils;[1]
Thy fair enchanted cup, and warbling charms[2]
No more on me have power, their force is nulled,

---

1 *I know thy … and toils* General terms from hunting for traps, snares, or lures.

2 *enchanted cup, and warbling charms* An allusion to Circe in Homer's *Odyssey*, whose magical potions turned Odysseus's men into pleasure-loving voluptuaries and then into swine; possibly also an allusion to the sirens, whose beautiful songs led men to their deaths.

So much of adder's wisdom[1] I have learnt
To fence my ear against thy sorceries.
If in my flower of youth and strength, when all men
Loved, honoured, feared me, thou alone could hate me
Thy husband, slight me, sell me, and forgo me;
How wouldst thou use me now, blind, and thereby
Deceivable, in most things as a child
Helpless, thence easily contemned, and scorned,
And last neglected? How wouldst thou insult
When I must live uxorious[2] to thy will
In perfect thraldom, how again betray me,
Bearing my words and doings to the lords
To gloss upon,[3] and censuring, frown or smile?
This jail I count the house of liberty
To thine[4] whose doors my feet shall never enter.
DALILA. Let me approach at least, and touch thy hand.
SAMSON. Not for thy life, lest fierce remembrance wake
My sudden rage to tear thee joint by joint.
At distance I forgive thee, go with that;
Bewail thy falsehood, and the pious works
It hath brought forth to make thee memorable
Among illustrious women, faithful wives:
Cherish thy hastened widowhood with the gold
Of matrimonial treason: so farewell.
DALILA. I see thou art implacable, more deaf
To prayers, than winds and seas, yet winds to seas
Are reconciled at length, and sea to shore:
Thy anger, unappeasable, still rages,
Eternal tempest never to be calmed.
Why do I humble thus myself, and suing
For peace, reap nothing but repulse and hate?
Bid go with evil omen and the brand

---

1 *adder's wisdom* Deafness. The proverbial deafness of adders derived from Psalms 58.4–5: "they are like the deaf adder that stoppeth her ear; which will not hearken to the voice of charmers, charming never so wisely."

2 *uxorious* Excessively fond of or dependent on one's wife.

3 *To gloss upon* To interpret in their own way.

4 *To thine* Compared to yours.

Of infamy upon my name denounced?
To mix with thy concernments I desist
Henceforth, nor too much disapprove my own.
Fame if not double-faced is double-mouthed,
And with contrary blast proclaims most deeds,
On both his wings, one black, the other white,
Bears greatest names in his wild airy flight.
My name perhaps among the circumcised
In Dan,[1] in Judah, and the bordering tribes,
To all posterity may stand defamed,
With malediction mentioned, and the blot
Of falsehood most unconjugal traduced.° *maligned*
But in my country where I most desire,
In Ecron, Gaza, Asdod, and in Gath[2]
I shall be named among the famousest
Of women, sung at solemn festivals,
Living and dead recorded, who to save
Her country from a fierce destroyer, chose
Above the faith of wedlock-bands, my tomb
With odours visited and annual flowers.
Not less renowned than in Mount Ephraim,
Jael,[3] who with inhospitable guile
Smote Sisera sleeping through the temples nailed.
Nor shall I count it heinous to enjoy
The public marks of honour and reward
Conferred upon me, for the piety
Which to my country I was judged to have shown.
At this whoever envies or repines
I leave him to his lot, and like my own.

Chorus. She's gone, a manifest serpent by her sting
Discovered in the end, till now concealed.

---

1 *Dan* Home of the Danites, Samson's tribe.

2 *Ecron, Gaza, Asdod … Gath* Four of the five main Philistine cities.

3 *Jael* See Judges 4.17–24; Jael, the wife of Heber the Kenite, gave refuge to the Canaanite general Sisera as he fled an Israelite force led by Barak, but then murdered him as he slept by hammering a tent peg into his temple. She was praised in song by Deborah and Barak (Judges 5.24–31); Dalila imagines her people, the Philistines, celebrating her in similar fashion.

Samson. So let her go, God sent her to debase me,
And aggravate my folly who committed
To such a viper his most sacred trust
Of secrecy, my safety, and my life.
Chorus. Yet beauty, though injurious, hath strange power,
After offence returning, to regain
Love once possessed, nor can be easily
Repulsed, without much inward passion felt
And secret sting of amorous remorse.
Samson. Love-quarrels oft in pleasing concord end,
Not wedlock-treachery endangering life.
Chorus. It is not virtue, wisdom, valour, wit,
Strength, comeliness of shape, or amplest merit
That woman's love can win or long inherit;° *possess*
But what it is, hard is to say,
Harder to hit
(Which way soever men refer it),
Much like thy riddle,[1] Samson, in one day
Or seven, though one should musing sit;
If any of these or all, the Timnian bride
Had not so soon preferred
Thy paranymph,[2] worthless to thee compared,
Successor in thy bed,
Nor both so loosely disallied
Their nuptials, nor this last so treacherously
Had shorn the fatal harvest of thy head.
Is it for that such outward ornament
Was lavished on their sex, that inward gifts
Were left for haste unfinished, judgment scant,
Capacity not raised to apprehend
Or value what is best
In choice, but oftest to affect the wrong?
Or was too much of self-love mixed,
Of constancy no root infixed,

1 *thy riddle* See Judges 14.12–18.

2 *paranymph* Groomsman or "best man" at a wedding: see Judges 14.20, which is silent about the bride's preferences and indicates only that she was "given to" Samson's companion after Samson left her in anger.

That either they love nothing, or not long?
Whate'er it be, to wisest men and best
Seeming at first all heavenly under virgin veil,
Soft, modest, meek, demure,
Once joined, the contrary she proves, a thorn
Intestine,° far within defensive arms *internal*
A cleaving mischief, in his way to virtue
Adverse and turbulent, or by her charms
Draws him awry enslaved
With dotage,° and his sense depraved *infatuation*
To folly and shameful deeds which ruin ends.
What pilot so expert but needs must wreck
Embarked with such a steers-mate at the helm?
Favoured of heaven who finds
One virtuous rarely found,
That in domestic good combines:
Happy that house! His way to peace is smooth:
But virtue which breaks through all opposition,
And all temptation can remove,
Most shines and most is acceptable above.
Therefore God's universal law
Gave to the man despotic power
Over his female in due awe,
Nor from that right to part an hour,
Smile she or lour:
So shall he least confusion draw
On his whole life, not swayed
By female usurpation,[1] nor dismayed.
But had we best retire, I see a storm?
SAMSON. Fair days have oft contracted° wind and rain. *brought*
CHORUS. But this another kind of tempest brings.
SAMSON. Be less abstruse,° my riddling days are past. *obscure*
CHORUS. Look now for no enchanting voice, nor fear
The bait of honeyed words; a rougher tongue
Draws hitherward, I know him by his stride,

1 *not swayed ... usurpation* An allusion to 1 Timothy 2.12–13: "But I suffer not a woman to teach, nor to usurp authority over the man, but to be in silence."

The giant Harapha[1] of Gath, his look
Haughty as is his pile° high-built and proud. *building*
Comes he in peace? What wind hath blown him hither
I less conjecture than when first I saw
The sumptuous Dalila floating this way:
His habit carries peace, his brow defiance.
Samson. Or peace or not, alike to me he comes.
Chorus. His fraught° we soon shall know, he now arrives. *business*
Harapha. I come not Samson, to condole thy chance,
As these perhaps, yet wish it had not been,
Though for no friendly intent. I am of Gath,
Men call me Harapha, of stock renowned
As Og or Anak and the Emims old
That Kiriathaim[2] held, thou know'st me now
If thou at all art known.[3] Much I have heard
Of thy prodigious might and feats performed
Incredible to me, in this displeased,
That I was never present on the place
Of those encounters, where we might have tried
Each other's force in camp or listed field:[4]
And now am come to see of whom such noise
Hath walked about, and each limb to survey,
If thy appearance answer loud report.
Samson. The way to know were not to see but taste.
Harapha. Dost thou already single° me? I thought *challenge*
Gyves° and the mill had tamed thee. O that fortune *shackles*
Had brought me to the field where thou art famed
To have wrought such wonders with an ass's jaw;
I should have forced thee soon wish other arms,

---

1 *Harapha* Not in the biblical story of Samson, but modeled on Goliath; the name derives from the Hebrew word for giant.

2 *Og or Anak and the Emims* Biblical giants (Numbers 13.33, Deuteronomy 2.10–11, 3.11); *Kiriathaim* Home to the Emims (Genesis 14.5).

3 *thou know'st me ... art known* Echoing Satan in *Paradise Lost*, when Ithuriel and Zephon discover him in Eden and demand his identity: "Not to know me argues yourselves unknown" (4.830), Satan haughtily replies.

4 *camp or listed field* A camp is a field for battle, and a listed field is a tiltyard for tournaments.

Or left thy carcass where the ass lay thrown:
So had the glory of prowess been recovered
To Palestine, won by a Philistine
From the unforeskinned race, of whom thou bear'st
The highest name for valiant acts; that honour
Certain to have won by mortal duel from thee,
I lose, prevented by thy eyes put out.

SAMSON. Boast not of what thou wouldst have done, but do
What then thou wouldst, thou seest it in thy hand.

HARAPHA. To combat with a blind man I disdain,
And thou hast need much washing to be touched.

SAMSON. Such usage as your honourable lords
Afford me assassinated° and betrayed, *attacked treacherously*
Who durst not with their whole united powers
In fight withstand me single and unarmed,
Nor in the house with chamber ambushes
Close°-banded durst attack me, no not sleeping, *secretly*
Till they had hired a woman with their gold
Breaking her marriage faith to circumvent me.
Therefore without feigned shifts let be assigned
Some narrow place enclosed, where sight may give thee,
Or rather flight, no great advantage on me;
Then put on all thy gorgeous arms, thy helmet
And brigandine of brass, thy broad habergeon,
Vantbrace and greaves, and gauntlet,[1] add thy spear
A weaver's beam, and seven-times-folded shield,[2]
I only with an oaken staff will meet thee,
And raise such outcries on thy clattered iron,
Which long shall not withhold me from thy head,
That in a little time while breath remains thee,
Thou oft shalt wish thyself at Gath to boast
Again in safety what thou wouldst have done

---

1 *brigandine* Body armor; *habergeon* Sleeveless coat of mail; *Vantbrace* Armor for the forearm; *greaves* Armor for the shin; *gauntlet* Armor for the hand.

2 *weaver's beam* Large wooden roller on a loom; the comparison echoes the description of Goliath's spear in 1 Samuel 17.7; *seven-times-folded shield* Shield of oxhide folded seven times, like the shields of classical heroes Ajax (*Iliad* 7.220) and Turnus (*Aeneid* 12.925).

To Samson, but shalt never see Gath more.
Harapha. Thou durst not thus disparage glorious arms
Which greatest heroes have in battle worn,
Their ornament and safety, had not spells
And black enchantments, some magician's art
Armed thee or charmed thee strong, which thou from heaven
Feign'dst at thy birth was given thee in thy hair,
Where strength can least abide, though all thy hairs
Were bristles ranged like those that ridge the back
Of chafed wild boars or ruffled porcupines.
Samson. I know no spells, use no forbidden arts;
My trust is in the living God who gave me
At my nativity this strength, diffused
No less through all my sinews, joints and bones,
Than thine, while I preserved these locks unshorn,
The pledge of my unviolated vow.
For proof hereof, if Dagon be thy god,
Go to his temple, invocate his aid
With solemnest devotion, spread before him
How highly it concerns his glory now
To frustrate and dissolve these magic spells,
Which I to be the power of Israel's God
Avow, and challenge Dagon to the test,
Offering to combat thee his champion bold,
With the utmost of his godhead seconded:[1]
Then thou shalt see, or rather to thy sorrow
Soon feel, whose God is strongest, thine or mine.
Harapha. Presume not on thy God, whate'er he be,
Thee he regards not, owns not, hath cut off
Quite from his people, and delivered up
Into thy enemies' hand, permitted them
To put out both thine eyes, and fettered send thee
Into the common prison, there to grind
Among the slaves and asses thy comrades,
As good for nothing else, no better service
With those thy boisterous locks, no worthy match

1 *godhead* Divine nature; *seconded* Appointed to assist.

For valour to assail, nor by the sword
Of noble warrior, so to stain his honour,
But by the barber's razor best subdued.

SAMSON. All these indignities, for such they are
From thine, these evils I deserve and more,
Acknowledge them from God inflicted on me
Justly, yet despair not of his final pardon
Whose ear is ever open; and his eye
Gracious to readmit the suppliant;
In confidence whereof I once again
Defy thee to the trial of mortal fight,
By combat to decide whose god is God,
Thine or whom I with Israel's sons adore.

HARAPHA. Fair honour that thou dost thy God, in trusting
He will accept thee to defend his cause,
A murderer, a revolter, and a robber.

SAMSON. Tongue-doughty[1] giant, how dost thou prove me these?

HARAPHA. Is not thy nation subject to our lords?
Their magistrates confessed it, when they took thee
As a league°-breaker and delivered bound *alliance*
Into our hands: for hadst thou not committed
Notorious murder on those thirty men
At Ascalon, who never did thee harm,
Then like a robber stripp'dst them of their robes?
The Philistines, when thou hadst broke the league,
Went up with armèd powers thee only seeking,
To others did no violence nor spoil.

SAMSON. Among the daughters of the Philistines
I chose a wife, which argued me no foe;
And in your city held my nuptial feast:
But your ill-meaning politician lords,
Under pretence of bridal friends and guests,
Appointed to await me thirty spies,
Who threatening cruel death constrained the bride
To wring from me and tell to them my secret,
That solved the riddle which I had proposed.

---

1 *Tongue-doughty* Valiant in speech.

When I perceived all set on enmity,
As on my enemies, wherever chanced,
I used hostility, and took their spoil
To pay my underminers in their coin.
My nation was subjected to your lords.
It was the force of conquest; force with force
Is well ejected when the conquered can.
But I a private person, whom my country
As a league-breaker gave up bound, presumed
Single rebellion and did hostile acts.
I was no private but a person raised
With strength sufficient and command from heaven
To free my country; if their servile minds
Me their deliverer sent would not receive,
But to their masters gave me up for naught,
The unworthier they; whence to this day they serve.
I was to do my part from heaven assigned,
And had performed it if my known offence
Had not disabled me, not all your force:
These shifts refuted, answer thy appellant° *challenger*
Though by his blindness maimed for high attempts,
Who now defies thee thrice to single fight,
As a petty enterprise of small enforce.° *difficulty*
HARAPHA. With thee a man condemned, a slave enrolled,
Due by the law to capital punishment?
To fight with thee no man of arms will deign.
SAMSON. Cam'st thou for this, vain boaster, to survey me,
To descant° on my strength, and give thy verdict? *discourse*
Come nearer, part not hence so slight informed;
But take good heed my hand survey not thee.
HARAPHA. O Baal-zebub![1] Can my ears unused
Hear these dishonours, and not render death?
SAMSON. No man withholds thee, nothing from thy hand
Fear I incurable; bring up thy van,[2]
My heels are fettered, but my fist is free.

---

1 *Baal-zebub* A god of the Philistines.

2 *van* Vanguard, the foremost division of an army; i.e., start your attack.

Harapha. This insolence other kind of answer fits.
Samson. Go baffled° coward, lest I run upon thee, *disgraced*
Though in these chains, bulk without spirit vast,
And with one buffet lay thy structure low,
Or swing thee in the air, then dash thee down
To the hazard of thy brains and shattered sides.
Harapha. By Astaroth[1] ere long thou shalt lament
These braveries in irons loaden on thee.
Chorus. His giantship is gone somewhat crestfall'n,
Stalking with less unconscionable[2] strides,
And lower looks, but in a sultry chafe.
Samson. I dread him not, nor all his giant-brood,
Though fame divulge him father of five sons
All of gigantic size, Goliah[3] chief.
Chorus. He will directly to the lords, I fear,
And with malicious counsel stir them up
Some way or other yet further to afflict thee.
Samson. He must allege some cause, and offered fight
Will not dare mention, lest a question rise
Whether he durst accept the offer or not,
And that he durst not plain enough appeared.
Much more affliction than already felt
They cannot well impose, nor I sustain;
If they intend advantage of my labours,
The work of many hands, which earns my keeping
With no small profit daily to my owners.
But come what will, my deadliest foe will prove
My speediest friend, by death to rid me hence,
The worst that he can give, to me the best.
Yet so it may fall out, because their end
Is hate, not help to me, it may with mine
Draw their own ruin who attempt the deed.
Chorus. Oh how comely it is and how reviving
To the spirits of just men long oppressed!
When God into the hands of their deliverer

---

1 *Astaroth* Ancient goddess (also Ashtoreth, Astarte, Ishtar, etc.).

2 *less unconscionable* Less excessive, shorter.

3 *Goliah* Goliath (see 1 Samuel 17 and 2 Samuel 19–22).

Puts invincible might
To quell the mighty of the earth, the oppressor,
The brute and boisterous force of violent men
Hardy and industrious to support
Tyrannic power, but raging to pursue
The righteous and all such as honour truth;
He all their ammunition
And feats of war defeats
With plain heroic magnitude of mind
And celestial vigour armed,
Their armouries and magazines contemns,
Renders them useless, while
With wingèd expedition° *speed*
Swift as the lightning glance he executes
His errand on the wicked, who surprised
Lose their defence distracted and amazed.
But patience is more oft the exercise
Of saints, the trial of their fortitude,
Making them each his own deliverer,
And victor over all
That tyranny or fortune can inflict;
Either of these is in thy lot,
Samson, with might endued
Above the sons of men; but sight bereaved
May chance to number thee with those
Whom patience finally must crown.
This idol's day hath been to thee no day of rest,
Labouring thy mind
More than the working day thy hands,
And yet perhaps more trouble is behind.
For I descry this way
Some other tending, in his hand
A sceptre or quaint° staff he bears, *strange*
Comes on amain, speed in his look.
By his habit° I discern him now *clothing*
A public officer, and now at hand.
His message will be short and voluble.° *rapid*

OFFICER. Hebrews, the prisoner Samson here I seek.

Chorus. His manacles remark him,[1] there he sits.
Officer. Samson, to thee our lords thus bid me say:
This day to Dagon is a solemn feast,
With sacrifices, triumph, pomp, and games;
Thy strength they know surpassing human rate,
And now some public proof thereof require
To honour this great feast, and great assembly;
Rise therefore with all speed and come along,
Where I will see thee heartened and fresh clad
To appear as fits before the illustrious lords.
Samson. Thou know'st I am an Hebrew, therefore tell them,
Our law forbids at their religious rites
My presence; for that cause I cannot come.
Officer. This answer, be assured, will not content them.
Samson. Have they not sword-players, and every sort
Of gymnic artists, wrestlers, riders, runners,
Jugglers and dancers, antics, mummers,[2] mimics,
But they must pick me out with shackles tired,
And over-laboured at their public mill,
To make them sport with blind activity?
Do they not seek occasion of new quarrels
On my refusal to distress me more,
Or make a game of my calamities?
Return the way thou cam'st, I will not come.
Officer. Regard thyself, this will offend them highly.
Samson. Myself? My conscience and internal peace.
Can they think me so broken, so debased
With corporal servitude, that my mind ever
Will condescend to such absurd commands?
Although their drudge, to be their fool or jester,
And in my midst of sorrow and heart-grief
To show them feats, and play before their god,
The worst of all indignities, yet on me
Joined° with extreme contempt? I will not come. *enjoined*

---

1 *remark him* Make him noticeable.

2 *Jugglers and … mummers* The word *jugglers* originally referred to jesters; *antics* Buffoons or clowns who act in a grotesque manner; *mummers* Masked performers in a traditional mime.

OFFICER. My message was imposed on me with speed,
Brooks no delay: is this thy resolution?
SAMSON. So take it with what speed thy message needs.
OFFICER. I am sorry what this stoutness° will produce. *determination*
SAMSON. Perhaps thou shalt have cause to sorrow indeed.
CHORUS. Consider, Samson; matters now are strained
Up to the highth, whether to hold or break;
He's gone, and who knows how he may report
Thy words by adding fuel to the flame?
Expect another message more imperious,
More lordly thundering than thou well wilt bear.
SAMSON. Shall I abuse this consecrated gift
Of strength, again returning with my hair
After my great transgression, so requite
Favour renewed, and add a greater sin
By prostituting holy things to idols;
A Nazarite in place abominable
Vaunting my strength in honour to their Dagon?
Besides, how vile, contemptible, ridiculous,
What act more execrably unclean, profane?
CHORUS. Yet with this strength thou serv'st the Philistines,
Idolatrous, uncircumcised, unclean.
SAMSON. Not in their idol-worship, but by labour
Honest and lawful to deserve my food
Of those who have me in their civil power.
CHORUS. Where the heart joins not, outward acts defile not.
SAMSON. Where outward force constrains, the sentence° holds: *maxim*
But who constrains me to the temple of Dagon,
Not dragging? The Philistian lords command.
Commands are no constraints. If I obey them,
I do it freely; venturing to displease
God for the fear of man, and man prefer,
Set God behind: which in his jealousy
Shall never, unrepented, find forgiveness.
Yet that he may dispense with[1] me or thee

1 *dispense with* Offer dispensation to, excuse, tolerate.

Present in temples at idolatrous rites
For some important cause, thou need'st not doubt.
CHORUS. How thou wilt here come off surmounts my reach.
SAMSON. Be of good courage, I begin to feel
Some rousing motions in me which dispose
To something extraordinary my thoughts.
I with this messenger will go along,
Nothing to do, be sure, that may dishonour
Our law, or stain my vow of Nazarite.
If there be aught of presage in the mind,
This day will be remarkable in my life
By some great act, or of my days the last.
CHORUS. In time thou hast resolved, the man returns.
OFFICER. Samson, this second message from our lords
To thee I am bid say. Art thou our slave,
Our captive, at the public mill our drudge,
And dar'st thou at our sending and command
Dispute thy coming? Come without delay;
Or we shall find such engines[1] to assail
And hamper thee, as thou shalt come of force,
Though thou wert firmlier fastened than a rock.
SAMSON. I could be well content to try their art,
Which to no few of them would prove pernicious.
Yet knowing their advantages too many,
Because they shall not trail me through their streets
Like a wild beast, I am content to go.
Masters' commands come with a power resistless
To such as owe them absolute subjection;
And for a life who will not change his purpose?
(So mutable are all the ways of men)
Yet this be sure, in nothing to comply
Scandalous or forbidden in our law.
OFFICER. I praise thy resolution, doff these links:
By this compliance thou wilt win the lords
To favour, and perhaps to set thee free.

---

1 *engines* Instruments of torture.

Samson. Brethren farewell, your company along
I will not wish, lest it perhaps offend them
To see me girt with friends; and how the sight
Of me as of a common enemy,
So dreaded once, may now exasperate them
I know not. Lords are lordliest in their wine;
And the well-feasted priest then soonest fired
With zeal, if aught religion seem concerned:
No less the people on their holy-days
Impetuous, insolent, unquenchable;
Happen what may, of me expect to hear
Nothing dishonourable, impure, unworthy
Our God, our law, my nation, or my self,
The last of me or no I cannot warrant.
Chorus. Go, and the Holy One
Of Israel be thy guide
To what may serve his glory best, and spread his name
Great among the heathen round:
Send thee the angel of thy birth, to stand
Fast by thy side, who from thy father's field
Rode up in flames after his message told
Of thy conception, and be now a shield
Of fire; that spirit that first rushed on thee
In the camp of Dan
Be efficacious in thee now at need.
For never was from heaven imparted
Measure of strength so great to mortal seed,
As in thy wondrous actions hath been seen.
But wherefore comes old Manoa in such haste
With youthful steps? Much livelier than erewhile
He seems: supposing here to find his son,
Or of him bringing to us some glad news?
Manoa. Peace with you brethren; my inducement hither
Was not at present here to find my son,
By order of the lords new parted hence
To come and play before them at their feast.
I heard all as I came, the city rings
And numbers thither flock, I had no will,

Lest I should see him forced to things unseemly.
But that which moved my coming now, was chiefly
To give ye part with me[1] what hope I have
With good success to work his liberty.
CHORUS. That hope would much rejoice us to partake
With thee; say reverend sire, we thirst to hear.
MANOA. I have attempted one by one the lords
Either at home, or through the high street passing,
With supplication prone and father's tears
To accept of ransom for my son their prisoner,
Some much averse I found and wondrous harsh,
Contemptuous, proud, set on revenge and spite;
That part most reverenced Dagon and his priests,
Others more moderate seeming, but their aim
Private reward, for which both god and state
They easily would set to sale; a third
More generous far and civil, who confessed
They had enough revenged, having reduced
Their foe to misery beneath their fears,
The rest was magnanimity to remit,
If some convenient° ransom were proposed. *suitable*
What noise or shout was that? It tore the sky.
CHORUS. Doubtless the people shouting to behold
Their once great dread, captive, and blind before them,
Or at some proof of strength before them shown.
MANOA. His ransom, if my whole inheritance
May compass it, shall willingly be paid
And numbered down: much rather I shall choose
To live the poorest in my tribe, than richest,
And he in that calamitous prison left.
No, I am fixed not to part hence without him.
For his redemption all my patrimony,
If need be, I am ready to forgo
And quit: not wanting him, I shall want nothing.
CHORUS. Fathers are wont to lay up for their sons,
Thou for thy son art bent to lay out all;

1 *give ye part with me* Impart or tell to you.

Sons wont to nurse their parents in old age,
Thou in old age car'st how to nurse thy son,
Made older than thy age through eyesight lost.
Manoa. It shall be my delight to tend his eyes,
And view him sitting in the house, ennobled
With all those high exploits by him achieved,
And on his shoulders waving down those locks,
That of a nation armed the strength contained:
And I persuade me God had not permitted
His strength again to grow up with his hair
Garrisoned round about him like a camp
Of faithful soldiery, were not his purpose
To use him further yet in some great service,
Not to sit idle with so great a gift
Useless, and thence ridiculous about him.
And since his strength with eyesight was not lost,
God will restore him eyesight to his strength.
Chorus. Thy hopes are not ill founded nor seem vain
Of his delivery, and thy joy thereon
Conceived, agreeable to a father's love,
In both which we, as next,[1] participate.
Manoa. I know your friendly minds and—O what noise!
Mercy of heaven what hideous noise was that!
Horribly loud unlike the former shout.
Chorus. Noise call you it or universal groan
As if the whole inhabitation perished,
Blood, death, and deathful deeds are in that noise,
Ruin, destruction at the utmost point.
Manoa. Of ruin[2] indeed methought I heard the noise,
O it continues, they have slain my son.
Chorus. Thy son is rather slaying them, that outcry
From slaughter of one foe could not ascend.
Manoa. Some dismal accident it needs must be;
What shall we do, stay here or run and see?

---

1 *as next* As next of kin (as fellow Danites).

2 *ruin* With the Latin sense of fall or collapse (as of a building).

Chorus. Best keep together here, lest running thither
We unawares run into danger's mouth.
This evil on the Philistines is fall'n,
From whom could else a general cry be heard?
The sufferers then will scarce molest us here,
From other hands we need not much to fear.
What if his eyesight (for to Israel's God
Nothing is hard) by miracle restored,
He now be dealing dole° among his foes, *sorrow*
And over heaps of slaughtered walk his way?
Manoa. That were a joy presumptuous to be thought.
Chorus. Yet God hath wrought things as incredible
For his people of old; what hinders now?
Manoa. He can I know, but doubt to think he will;
Yet hope would fain subscribe, and tempts belief.
A little stay will bring some notice hither.
Chorus. Of good or bad so great, of bad the sooner;
For evil news rides post, while good news baits.° *travels slowly*
And to our wish I see one hither speeding,
An Hebrew, as I guess, and of our tribe.
Messenger. O whither shall I run, or which way fly
The sight of this so horrid spectacle
Which erst my eyes beheld and yet behold;
For dire imagination still pursues me.
But providence or instinct of nature seems,
Or reason though disturbed, and scarce consulted
To have guided me aright, I know not how,
To thee first reverend Manoa, and to these
My countrymen, whom here I knew remaining,
As at some distance from the place of horror,
So in the sad event too much concerned.
Manoa. The accident was loud, and here before thee
With rueful cry, yet what it was we hear not,
No preface needs, thou seest we long to know.
Messenger. It would burst forth, but I recover breath
And sense distract, to know well what I utter.
Manoa. Tell us the sum, the circumstance defer.

Messenger. Gaza yet stands, but all her sons are fall'n,
All in a moment overwhelmed and fall'n.
Manoa. Sad, but thou know'st to Israelites not saddest
The desolation of a hostile city.
Messenger. Feed on that first, there may in grief be surfeit.
Manoa. Relate by whom.
Messenger. By Samson.
Manoa. That still lessens
The sorrow, and converts it nigh to joy.
Messenger. Ah Manoa I refrain, too suddenly
To utter what will come at last too soon;
Lest evil tidings with too rude irruption
Hitting thy agèd ear should pierce too deep.
Manoa. Suspense in news is torture, speak them out.
Messenger. Then take the worst in brief, Samson is dead.
Manoa. The worst indeed, O all my hope's defeated
To free him hence! But death who sets all free
Hath paid his ransom now and full discharge.
What windy joy this day had I conceived
Hopeful of his delivery, which now proves
Abortive as the first-born bloom of spring
Nipped with the lagging rear of winter's frost.
Yet ere I give the reins to grief, say first,
How died he? Death to life is crown or shame.
All by him fell thou say'st, by whom fell he,
What glorious hand gave Samson his death's wound?
Messenger. Unwounded of his enemies he fell.
Manoa. Wearied with slaughter then or how? Explain.
Messenger. By his own hands.
Manoa. Self-violence? What cause
Brought him so soon at variance with himself
Among his foes?
Messenger. Inevitable cause
At once both to destroy and be destroyed;
The edifice where all were met to see him
Upon their heads and on his own he pulled.
Manoa. O lastly over-strong against thyself!
A dreadful way thou took'st to thy revenge.

More than enough we know; but while things yet
Are in confusion, give us if thou canst,
Eye-witness of what first or last was done,
Relation more particular and distinct.

Messenger. Occasions drew me early to this city,
And as the gates I entered with sunrise,
The morning trumpets festival proclaimed
Through each high street: little I had dispatched
When all abroad was rumoured that this day
Samson should be brought forth to show the people
Proof of his mighty strength in feats and games;
I sorrowed at his captive state, but minded
Not to be absent at that spectacle.
The building was a spacious theatre
Half round on two main pillars vaulted high,
With seats where all the lords and each degree
Of sort,° might sit in order to behold; *rank*
The other side was open, where the throng
On banks and scaffolds under sky might stand;[1]
I among these aloof obscurely stood.
The feast and noon grew high, and sacrifice
Had filled their hearts with mirth, high cheer, and wine,
When to their sports they turned. Immediately
Was Samson as a public servant brought,
In their state livery clad; before him pipes
And timbrels, on each side went armèd guards,
Both horse and foot before him and behind
Archers, and slingers, cataphracts and spears.[2]
At sight of him the people with a shout
Rifted the air clamouring their god with praise,
Who had made their dreadful enemy their thrall.
He patient but undaunted where they led him,
Came to the place, and what was set before him
Which without help of eye might be assayed,

---

1 *The other side … stand* See Judges 16.27 and line 1659 below. In the biblical account, the general audience of men and women sits on the building's roof (and so dies when Samson pulls down the pillars).

2 *cataphracts* Armored soldiers; *spears* Spearmen.

To heave, pull, draw, or break, he still performed
All with incredible, stupendious force,
None daring to appear antagonist.
At length for intermission sake they led him
Between the pillars; he his guide requested
(For so from such as nearer stood we heard)
As over-tired to let him lean a while
With both his arms on those two massy pillars
That to the archèd roof gave main support.
He unsuspicious led him; which when Samson
Felt in his arms, with head a while inclined,
And eyes fast fixed he stood, as one who prayed,
Or some great matter in his mind revolved.
At last with head erect thus cried aloud,
Hitherto, lords, what your commands imposed
I have performed, as reason was, obeying,
Not without wonder or delight beheld.
Now of my own accord such other trial
I mean to show you of my strength, yet greater;
As with amaze shall strike all who behold.
This uttered, straining all his nerves he bowed,
As with the force of winds and waters pent,
When mountains tremble, those two massy pillars
With horrible convulsion to and fro,
He tugged, he shook, till down they came and drew
The whole roof after them, with burst of thunder
Upon the heads of all who sat beneath,
Lords, ladies, captains, counsellors, or priests,
Their choice nobility and flower, not only
Of this but each Philistian city round
Met from all parts to solemnize this feast.
Samson with these immixed, inevitably
Pulled down the same destruction on himself;
The vulgar[1] only scaped who stood without.

---

1 *vulgar* Common people. See Judges 16.28–31 and lines 1609–10 above; Milton alters the biblical account by restricting the slaughter to the Philistines' social, political, military, and religious elite.

CHORUS. O dearly-bought revenge, yet glorious!
Living or dying thou hast fulfilled
The work for which thou wast foretold
To Israel, and now li'st victorious
Among thy slain self-killed
Not willingly, but tangled in the fold,
Of dire necessity, whose law in death conjoined
Thee with thy slaughtered foes in number more
Than all thy life had slain before.
SEMICHORUS. While their hearts were jocund and sublime,
Drunk with idolatry, drunk with wine,
And fat regorged of bulls and goats,
Chanting their idol, and preferring
Before our living dread[1] who dwells
In Silo[2] his bright sanctuary:
Among them he a spirit of frenzy sent,
Who hurt their minds,
And urged them on with mad desire
To call in haste for their destroyer;
They only set on sport and play
Unweetingly° importuned *unwittingly*
Their own destruction to come speedy upon them.
So fond are mortal men
Fall'n into wrath divine,
As their own ruin on themselves to invite,
Insensate left, or to sense reprobate,
And with blindness internal struck.
SEMICHORUS. But he though blind of sight,
Despised and thought extinguished quite,
With inward eyes illuminated
His fiery virtue roused
From under ashes into sudden flame,
And as an evening dragon[3] came,
Assailant on the perchèd roosts,

1 *dread* Object of deep reverence.

2 *Silo* Shiloh, a city of the Ephraimites.

3 *as an evening dragon* Like a serpent, assailing roosting fowl despite the darkness of night.

And nests in order ranged
Of tame villatic° fowl; but as an eagle *barnyard*
His cloudless thunder bolted on their heads.
So virtue given for lost,
Depressed, and overthrown, as seemed,
Like that self-begotten bird
In the Arabian woods embossed,
That no second knows nor third,
And lay erewhile a holocaust,
From out her ashy womb now teemed,
Revives, reflourishes, then vigorous most
When most unactive deemed,
And though her body die, her fame survives,
A secular bird ages of lives.[1]
MANOA. Come, come, no time for lamentation now,
Nor much more cause, Samson hath quit° himself *acquitted*
Like Samson, and heroically hath finished
A life heroic, on his enemies
Fully revenged, hath left them years of mourning,
And lamentation to the sons of Caphtor[2]
Through all Philistian bounds. To Israel
Honour hath left, and freedom, let but them
Find courage to lay hold on this occasion,
To himself and father's house eternal fame;
And which is best and happiest yet, all this
With God not parted from him, as was feared,
But favouring and assisting to the end.
Nothing is here for tears, nothing to wail
Or knock the breast, no weakness, no contempt,
Dispraise, or blame, nothing but well and fair,
And what may quiet us in a death so noble.
Let us go find the body where it lies
Soaked in his enemies' blood, and from the stream

---

1 *self-begotten bird ... of lives* The phoenix, supposed as existing only one at a time and reborn periodically out of its own ashes; *embossed* Imbosked, hidden in a wood; *holocaust* Sacrifice consumed by fire; *secular* Living for an age or ages.

2 *sons of Caphtor* The Philistines, described in the Bible as coming originally from a place called Caphtor.

With lavers° pure, and cleansing herbs wash off *washbasins*
The clotted gore. I with what speed the while
(Gaza is not in plight to say us nay)
Will send for all my kindred, all my friends
To fetch him hence and solemnly attend
With silent obsequy and funeral train
Home to his father's house: there will I build him
A monument, and plant it round with shade
Of laurel ever green, and branching palm,
With all his trophies hung, and acts enrolled
In copious legend, or sweet lyric song.
Thither shall all the valiant youth resort,
And from his memory inflame their breasts
To matchless valour, and adventures high:
The virgins also shall on feastful days
Visit his tomb with flowers, only bewailing
His lot unfortunate in nuptial choice,
From whence captivity and loss of eyes.
Chorus. All is best, though we oft doubt,
What the unsearchable dispose
Of highest wisdom brings about,
And ever best found in the close.
Oft he seems to hide his face,
But unexpectedly returns
And to his faithful champion hath in place
Bore witness gloriously; whence Gaza mourns
And all that band them to resist
His uncontrollable intent,
His servants he with new acquist° *acquisition*
Of true experience from this great event
With peace and consolation hath dismissed,
And calm of mind all passion spent.

—1671

In Context

The Biblical Version of the Samson Story

The primary source for *Samson Agonistes* is the account of Samson's life as presented in Judges 13–16. Milton dramatizes the account, focusing the poem's narrative "present" on a relatively short passage (Judges 16.21–30) but drawing freely on details elsewhere in the biblical narrative. A careful comparison of the biblical text with Milton's version of the story raises many interesting interpretative questions. The version presented here is the King James or Authorized translation, first published in 1611, though Milton was familiar with a wide range of versions and commentaries in various languages, including the original Hebrew.

Judges 13–16

13 And the children of Israel did evil again in the sight of the
LORD; and the LORD delivered them into the hand of the Philis-
tines forty years.
2 And there was a certain man of Zorah, of the family of the Dan-
ites, whose name was Manoah; and his wife was barren, and bare not.
3 And the angel of the LORD appeared unto the woman, and said
unto her, Behold now, thou art barren, and bearest not: but thou shalt
conceive, and bear a son. 4 Now therefore beware, I pray thee, and
drink not wine nor strong drink, and eat not any unclean thing: 5 For,
lo, thou shalt conceive, and bear a son; and no razor shall come on
his head: for the child shall be a Nazarite unto God from the womb:
and he shall begin to deliver Israel out of the hand of the Philistines.
6 Then the woman came and told her husband, saying, A man of God
came unto me, and his countenance was like the countenance of an
angel of God, very terrible: but I asked him not whence he was, nei-
ther told he me his name: 7 But he said unto me, Behold, thou shalt

conceive, and bear a son; and now drink no wine nor strong drink,
neither eat any unclean thing: for the child shall be a Nazarite to God
from the womb to the day of his death.

8 Then Manoah intreated the LORD, and said, O my Lord, let the
man of God which thou didst send come again unto us, and teach
us what we shall do unto the child that shall be born. 9 And God
hearkened to the voice of Manoah; and the angel of God came again
unto the woman as she sat in the field: but Manoah her husband was
not with her. 10 And the woman made haste, and ran, and shewed
her husband, and said unto him, Behold, the man hath appeared
unto me, that came unto me the other day. 11 And Manoah arose,
and went after his wife, and came to the man, and said unto him,
Art thou the man that spakest unto the woman? And he said, I am.
12 And Manoah said, Now let thy words come to pass. How shall we
order the child, and how shall we do unto him? 13 And the angel of
the LORD said unto Manoah, Of all that I said unto the woman let
her beware. 14 She may not eat of any thing that cometh of the vine,
neither let her drink wine or strong drink, nor eat any unclean thing:
all that I commanded her let her observe.

15 And Manoah said unto the angel of the LORD, I pray thee, let
us detain thee, until we shall have made ready a kid for thee. 16 And
the angel of the LORD said unto Manoah, Though thou detain me, I
will not eat of thy bread: and if thou wilt offer a burnt offering, thou
must offer it unto the LORD. For Manoah knew not that he was
an angel of the LORD. 17 And Manoah said unto the angel of the
LORD, What is thy name, that when thy sayings come to pass we
may do thee honour? 18 And the angel of the LORD said unto him,
Why askest thou thus after my name, seeing it is secret? 19 So Manoah
took a kid with a meat offering, and offered it upon a rock unto the
LORD: and the angel did wonderously; and Manoah and his wife
looked on. 20 For it came to pass, when the flame went up toward
heaven from off the altar, that the angel of the LORD ascended in the
flame of the altar. And Manoah and his wife looked on it, and fell on
their faces to the ground.

21 But the angel of the LORD did no more appear to Manoah
and to his wife. Then Manoah knew that he was an angel of the
LORD. 22 And Manoah said unto his wife, We shall surely die, be-
cause we have seen God. 23 But his wife said unto him, If the LORD

were pleased to kill us, he would not have received a burnt offering
and a meat offering at our hands, neither would he have shewed us
all these things, nor would as at this time have told us such things as
these. 24 And the woman bare a son, and called his name Samson:
and the child grew, and the LORD blessed him. 25 And the Spirit of
the LORD began to move him at times in the camp of Dan between
Zorah and Eshtaol.

14 And Samson went down to Timnath, and saw a woman in
Timnath of the daughters of the Philistines. 2 And he came up, and
told his father and his mother, and said, I have seen a woman in
Timnath of the daughters of the Philistines: now therefore get her
for me to wife. 3 Then his father and his mother said unto him, Is
there never a woman among the daughters of thy brethren, or among
all my people, that thou goest to take a wife of the uncircumcised
Philistines? And Samson said unto his father, Get her for me; for she
pleaseth me well.

4 But his father and his mother knew not that it was of the LORD,
that he sought an occasion against the Philistines: for at that time the
Philistines had dominion over Israel.

5 Then went Samson down, and his father and his mother, to
Timnath, and came to the vineyards of Timnath: and, behold, a
young lion roared against him. 6 And the Spirit of the LORD came
mightily upon him, and he rent him as he would have rent a kid,
and he had nothing in his hand: but he told not his father or his
mother what he had done. 7 And he went down, and talked with the
woman; and she pleased Samson well. 8 And after a time he returned
to take her, and he turned aside to see the carcase of the lion: and,
behold, there was a swarm of bees and honey in the carcase of the
lion. 9 And he took thereof in his hands, and went on eating, and
came to his father and mother, and he gave them, and they did eat:
but he told not them that he had taken the honey out of the carcase
of the lion.

10 So his father went down unto the woman: and Samson made
there a feast; for so used the young men to do. 11 And it came to pass,
when they saw him, that they brought thirty companions to be with
him. 12 And Samson said unto them, I will now put forth a riddle
unto you: if ye can certainly declare it me within the seven days of
the feast, and find it out, then I will give you thirty sheets and thirty

change of garments: 13 But if ye cannot declare it me, then shall ye
give me thirty sheets and thirty change of garments. And they said
unto him, Put forth thy riddle, that we may hear it. 14 And he said
unto them,

> Out of the eater came forth meat,
> and out of the strong came forth sweetness.

And they could not in three days expound the riddle.
15 And it came to pass on the seventh day, that they said unto Sam-
son's wife, Entice thy husband, that he may declare unto us the riddle,
lest we burn thee and thy father's house with fire: have ye called us
to take that we have? is it not so? 16 And Samson's wife wept before
him, and said, Thou dost but hate me, and lovest me not: thou hast
put forth a riddle unto the children of my people, and hast not told
it me. And he said unto her, Behold, I have not told it my father nor
my mother, and shall I tell it thee? 17 And she wept before him the
seven days, while their feast lasted: and it came to pass on the seventh
day, that he told her, because she lay sore upon him: and she told the
riddle to the children of her people. 18 And the men of the city said
unto him on the seventh day before the sun went down,

> What is sweeter than honey?
> And what is stronger than a lion?

And he said unto them,

> If ye had not plowed with my heifer,
> ye had not found out my riddle.

19 And the Spirit of the LORD came upon him, and he went down
to Ashkelon, and slew thirty men of them, and took their spoil, and
gave change of garments unto them which expounded the riddle.
And his anger was kindled, and he went up to his father's house.
20 But Samson's wife was given to his companion, whom he had used
as his friend.

15 But it came to pass within a while after, in the time of wheat
harvest, that Samson visited his wife with a kid; and he said, I will go

in to my wife into the chamber. But her father would not suffer him
to go in. 2 And her father said, I verily thought that thou hadst utterly
hated her; therefore I gave her to thy companion: is not her younger
sister fairer than she? take her, I pray thee, instead of her. 3 And Sam-
son said concerning them, Now shall I be more blameless than the
Philistines, though I do them a displeasure. 4 And Samson went and
caught three hundred foxes, and took firebrands, and turned tail to
tail, and put a firebrand in the midst between two tails. 5 And when
he had set the brands on fire, he let them go into the standing corn of
the Philistines, and burnt up both the shocks, and also the standing
corn, with the vineyards and olives. 6 Then the Philistines said, Who
hath done this? And they answered, Samson, the son in law of the
Timnite, because he had taken his wife, and given her to his compan-
ion. And the Philistines came up, and burnt her and her father with
fire. 7 And Samson said unto them, Though ye have done this, yet will
I be avenged of you, and after that I will cease. 8 And he smote them
hip and thigh with a great slaughter: and he went down and dwelt in
the top of the rock Etam.

9 Then the Philistines went up, and pitched in Judah, and spread
themselves in Lehi. 10 And the men of Judah said, Why are ye come
up against us? And they answered, To bind Samson are we come up,
to do to him as he hath done to us. 11 Then three thousand men of
Judah went to the top of the rock Etam, and said to Samson, Knowest
thou not that the Philistines are rulers over us? what is this that thou
hast done unto us? And he said unto them, As they did unto me, so
have I done unto them. 12 And they said unto him, We are come
down to bind thee, that we may deliver thee into the hand of the
Philistines. And Samson said unto them, Swear unto me, that ye will
not fall upon me yourselves. 13 And they spake unto him, saying, No;
but we will bind thee fast, and deliver thee into their hand: but surely
we will not kill thee. And they bound him with two new cords, and
brought him up from the rock.

14 And when he came unto Lehi, the Philistines shouted against
him: and the Spirit of the LORD came mightily upon him, and the
cords that were upon his arms became as flax that was burnt with
fire, and his bands loosed from off his hands. 15 And he found a new
jawbone of an ass, and put forth his hand, and took it, and slew a
thousand men therewith. 16 And Samson said,

With the jawbone of an ass,
heaps upon heaps,
with the jaw of an ass
have I slain a thousand men.

17 And it came to pass, when he had made an end of speaking, that
he cast away the jawbone out of his hand, and called that place
Ramathlehi.

18 And he was sore athirst, and called on the LORD, and said,
Thou hast given this great deliverance into the hand of thy servant:
and now shall I die for thirst, and fall into the hand of the uncir-
cumcised? 19 But God clave an hollow place that was in the jaw, and
there came water thereout; and when he had drunk, his spirit came
again, and he revived: wherefore he called the name thereof Enhak-
kore, which is in Lehi unto this day. 20 And he judged Israel in the
days of the Philistines twenty years.

16 Then went Samson to Gaza, and saw there an harlot, and went
in unto her. 2 And it was told the Gazites, saying, Samson is come
hither. And they compassed him in, and laid wait for him all night in
the gate of the city, and were quiet all the night, saying, In the morn-
ing, when it is day, we shall kill him. 3 And Samson lay till midnight,
and arose at midnight, and took the doors of the gate of the city, and
the two posts, and went away with them, bar and all, and put them
upon his shoulders, and carried them up to the top of an hill that is
before Hebron.

4 And it came to pass afterward, that he loved a woman in the
valley of Sorek, whose name was Delilah. 5 And the lords of the Phil-
istines came up unto her, and said unto her, Entice him, and see
wherein his great strength lieth, and by what means we may prevail
against him, that we may bind him to afflict him; and we will give
thee every one of us eleven hundred pieces of silver. 6 And Delilah
said to Samson, Tell me, I pray thee, wherein thy great strength lieth,
and wherewith thou mightest be bound to afflict thee. 7 And Samson
said unto her, If they bind me with seven green withes that were never
dried, then shall I be weak, and be as another man. 8 Then the lords
of the Philistines brought up to her seven green withes which had not
been dried, and she bound him with them. 9 Now there were men ly-
ing in wait, abiding with her in the chamber. And she said unto him,

The Philistines be upon thee, Samson. And he brake the withes, as a
thread of tow is broken when it toucheth the fire. So his strength was
not known.

10 And Delilah said unto Samson, Behold, thou hast mocked me,
and told me lies: now tell me, I pray thee, wherewith thou might-
est be bound. 11 And he said unto her, If they bind me fast with
new ropes that never were occupied, then shall I be weak, and be as
another man. 12 Delilah therefore took new ropes, and bound him
therewith, and said unto him, The Philistines be upon thee, Samson.
And there were liers in wait abiding in the chamber. And he brake
them from off his arms like a thread.

13 And Delilah said unto Samson, Hitherto thou hast mocked me,
and told me lies: tell me wherewith thou mightest be bound. And
he said unto her, If thou weavest the seven locks of my head with
the web. 14 And she fastened it with the pin, and said unto him, The
Philistines be upon thee, Samson. And he awaked out of his sleep,
and went away with the pin of the beam, and with the web.

15 And she said unto him, How canst thou say, I love thee, when
thine heart is not with me? thou hast mocked me these three times,
and hast not told me wherein thy great strength lieth. 16 And it came
to pass, when she pressed him daily with her words, and urged him,
so that his soul was vexed unto death; 17 That he told her all his heart,
and said unto her, There hath not come a razor upon mine head; for
I have been a Nazarite unto God from my mother's womb: if I be
shaven, then my strength will go from me, and I shall become weak,
and be like any other man.

18 And when Delilah saw that he had told her all his heart, she sent
and called for the lords of the Philistines, saying, Come up this once,
for he hath shewed me all his heart. Then the lords of the Philistines
came up unto her, and brought money in their hand. 19 And she
made him sleep upon her knees; and she called for a man, and she
caused him to shave off the seven locks of his head; and she began
to afflict him, and his strength went from him. 20 And she said, The
Philistines be upon thee, Samson. And he awoke out of his sleep, and
said, I will go out as at other times before, and shake myself. And he
wist not that the LORD was departed from him. 21 But the Philis-
tines took him, and put out his eyes, and brought him down to Gaza,
and bound him with fetters of brass; and he did grind in the prison

house. 22 Howbeit the hair of his head began to grow again after he was shaven.

23 Then the lords of the Philistines gathered them together for to offer a great sacrifice unto Dagon their god, and to rejoice: for they said, Our god hath delivered Samson our enemy into our hand. 24 And when the people saw him, they praised their god: for they said, Our god hath delivered into our hands our enemy, and the destroyer of our country, which slew many of us. 25 And it came to pass, when their hearts were merry, that they said, Call for Samson, that he may make us sport. And they called for Samson out of the prison house; and he made them sport: and they set him between the pillars. 26 And Samson said unto the lad that held him by the hand, Suffer me that I may feel the pillars whereupon the house standeth, that I may lean upon them. 27 Now the house was full of men and women; and all the lords of the Philistines were there; and there were upon the roof about three thousand men and women, that beheld while Samson made sport.

28 And Samson called unto the LORD, and said, O Lord God, remember me, I pray thee, and strengthen me, I pray thee, only this once, O God, that I may be at once avenged of the Philistines for my two eyes. 29 And Samson took hold of the two middle pillars upon which the house stood, and on which it was borne up, of the one with his right hand, and of the other with his left. 30 And Samson said, Let me die with the Philistines. And he bowed himself with all his might; and the house fell upon the lords, and upon all the people that were therein. So the dead which he slew at his death were more than they which he slew in his life. 31 Then his brethren and all the house of his father came down, and took him, and brought him up, and buried him between Zorah and Eshtaol in the burying place of Manoah his father. And he judged Israel twenty years.

from the publisher

A name never says it all, but the word "broadview" expresses a good deal of the philosophy behind our company. We are open to a broad range of academic approaches and political viewpoints. We pay attention to the broad impact book publishing and book printing has in the wider world; we began using recycled stock more than a decade ago, and for some years now we have used 100% recycled paper for most titles. As a Canadian-based company we naturally publish a number of titles with a Canadian emphasis, but our publishing program overall is internationally oriented and broad-ranging. Our individual titles often appeal to a broad readership too; many are of interest as much to general readers as to academics and students.

Founded in 1985, Broadview remains a fully independent company owned by its shareholders—not an imprint or subsidiary of a larger multinational.

If you would like to find out more about Broadview and about the books we publish, please visit us at **www.broadviewpress.com**. And if you'd like to place an order through the site, we'd like to show our appreciation by extending a special discount to you: by entering the code below you will receive a 20% discount on purchases made through the Broadview website.

Discount code: **broadview20%**

Thank you for choosing Broadview.

Please note: this offer applies only to sales of bound books within the United States or Canada.

LIST

of products used:

799 lb(s) of Rolland Enviro100 Print
100% post-consumer

RESULTS

Based on the Cascades products you selected compared to products in the industry made with 100% virgin fiber, your savings are:

7 trees

6,552 gal. US of water
71 days of water consumption

670 lbs of waste
6 waste containers

2,202 lbs CO_2
4,176 miles driven

6 MMBTU
27,561 60W light bulbs for one hour

3 lbs NO_X
emissions of one truck during 4 days